Gardening on a
Shoestring

Gardening on a
Shoestring

Rob Proctor

Johnson Books
Boulder

Published by Johnson Books, a division of Big Earth Publishing,
3005 Center Green Drive, Suite 220, Boulder, Colorado 80301.
E-mail: books@bigearthpublishing.com
www.johnsonbooks.com

Cover and text design by Constance Bollen, cbgraphics

9   8   7   6   5   4   3   2   1

Library of Congress Cataloging-in-Publication Data
Proctor, Rob.
        Gardening on a shoestring / Rob Proctor
                p. cm.
Includes index.
        ISBN 1-55566-376-1
        1. Landscape gardening.   I. Title
SB473.P76   2006
635—dc22   2006005666

Printed in Malaysia

To my "little sister" Angie,
a sweet soul and a sturdy gardener

Acknowledgments

~

Thanks to Mira Perrizo for believing in this book, Marlene Blessing for editing it so gracefully, and Constance Bollen for making it beautiful. Additional thanks go to David Macke and Jeff Joyce for technical assistance, since I'm not known for my computer wizardry. And many more thanks to all my friends at Tagawa Garden Center, who love plants and animals.

Contents

My new home didn't have much going for it. Dull as dishwater, its sagging porch, aluminum siding, and scruffy lawn hinted at the horrors within. Three years later, its transformation is well under way. A six-year-old girl—strolling by with her mother—asked me recently, "Does Barbie live here?"

Introduction

Savvy real estate agents often advise their clients to buy the ugliest house on the block. I certainly did that. When I recently purchased a new home, I found a diamond in the rough—very rough. Entombed in '50s aluminum siding, this turn-of-the-(twentieth)-century farmhouse didn't have much curb appeal, from its sagging front porch to its scraggly lawn and graveled strip between the sidewalk and the street. The interior of the house was equally grim. A hundred years of "remuddling" had resulted in layers of beige sculptured pile on the floors, cheerful orange flowered wallpaper, and unsuccessful do-it-yourself cabinets, shelves, and tile work.

Turning this hovel into a home has been a challenge. The movie *The Money Pit* has new relevance for me now; what Tom Hanks and Shelley Long's characters went through seems only a slight exaggeration of the unanticipated remodeling problems that can lie in wait for homeowners. As a result, there hasn't been much cash to spend on making a new garden.

Perhaps you bought more wisely than I did, or your dream house came without nightmares. Even so, gardening can be incredibly expensive. If your front porch hasn't rotted, you may instead have the expense of orthodontists, ballet lessons, and hip new sneakers (and the children may need things as well).

Getting started can be daunting. What should I do first? What should I do next? Can I afford either one of these steps? If you answered "No," let's talk. Save money for the important things—fences, garden structures and furniture, pots, tools, and paving—and buy good, lasting, high-quality items. If you're the handy type, you can save bundles by building many of these things yourself.

The plant part is where you can accomplish a lot with a little cash. Nursery-grown plants can be pricey, and there are good reasons why. A gallon or quart perennial usually represents at least two years' work by the nursery staff, from the time the plant was started from seed, cutting, or division: costs include daily attention to watering and fertilization and the nursery's overhead—including propagators, clerks, accountants, and advertisers. And that doesn't even count energy costs, which can be staggering. I have no quarrel with the prices at the nursery—they are completely justified—but my ancient plumbing takes precedence over new perennials.

So how can a cash-strapped gardener achieve a beautiful garden? Mostly through your own labors. I removed my lawn by hand. All it took was time and several bottles of economy-size pain reliever. After I'd wiped the slate clean, it was time to plant. I formed a loose two-year plan. I spent a few hundred dollars for five-gallon shrubs—blue mist spirea, lilac, sand cherry, butterfly bush, and shrub roses. The money didn't go very far. I splurged an additional hundred dollars on young perennials. Foregoing the gallons, I concentrated on 3-inch and 2¼-inch containers. In the nursery trade such small containers are called "tuna quarters." This is the most economical way to buy, although some plants aren't available in these small sizes because of their extensive root systems. Peonies, ornamental grasses, yuccas, Japanese anemones, and monkshood are usually offered in gallon sizes and larger. (Nurseries usually order these plants in as "liners," bare-root two-year-old plants from wholesalers.)

Shopping end-of-season sales will also save you money. I love department store bargain basements; this is the green industry's equivalent. Your nursery would really like you to take their odd lots home so they don't have to deal with them over the winter. Shoppers can often save up to 50 percent. The selection will be a bit of a jumble and not what it was in spring, but bargains are the mother of creativity.

Seeds, of course, provide the least expensive way to grow a garden, usually at a fraction of the cost of nursery-grown plants. You supply the labor and overhead. It takes a few seasons to get the hang of growing from seed, both indoors and out. Eventually you'll start to "think" like a seed, gaining an intuitive sense of when and where to plant. Collecting seeds from your own garden and from friends saves further. Free is good. You must ask before you collect seed in any garden, especially a public one, which generally discourages it. Learning to take cuttings can also help you fill in your garden and pots. Fuchsias, geraniums, coleus, flowering maples, and many other plants are easy to propagate. Once again, with practice you'll get the hang of it.

Friends and neighbors are your best source of free plants. Usually, they're happy to share pieces of such plants as yarrow and iris. It's the way plants have been passed over the garden fence for generations. Just beware of any plant they're too happy to be rid of—it could be some invasive thing with the intent of conquering your garden. Shopping with bargain-conscious friends can also help you save bucks; buy a single plant you both like with the agreement to divide or take cuttings the next season. A small nursery bed, lavished with fertilizer and attention, can beef up small plants to share in a short time.

Collecting or buying plants economically isn't the only way to cut costs. Save your emptied pots and six packs. They're good for at least several seasons, until the plastic eventually becomes brittle. Rinse and run them through the dishwasher before planting seeds in them. A number of household items can be put to good use in growing and caring for your plants.

You can create yummy organic matter for beds and pots by composting garden debris and plant scraps. I save my potting soil from one year to the next, emptying patio pots in the fall and dumping the plants and soil in a pile. The roots and stems within break down and enrich the mixture when I turn it in the spring and add compost. Because I display hundreds of container plants on my patio, I need that soil to stretch. Rough compost, not yet fully decomposed, can be added to the bottom of each large pot to break down over the course of the summer. I even use my snow shovel in spring to scoop up crumbling leaves in the gutter and alley, which I mix into my potting soil.

There's yet one more way to fill a new garden. Treasure your "volunteer" seedlings. That's what I learned to call them as a kid. My mentor, Katie, our across-the-street neighbor who had the most magical garden ever, would say, "Oh, he just came up volunteer." My new garden, though just in its second year, depends on volunteerism. While there's a limit to what you can do with an overabundance of a handful of species, it's also sensible (and cheap) to grow what wants to grow for you. I cleared several hundred feet of that awful gravel on the parking strip (aka the "hellstrip") and I transplanted my volunteers to rapidly fill it in. Though I'd prefer a bit more plant diversity, I'm thrilled with the water-thrifty patchwork quilt of

This morning glory–covered trellis cost less than a hundred dollars at a discount store and the ceramic birdbath was a gift from friends.

meadow sage, snow daisy, ponytail grass, and lamb's ears, spiced by more than a hundred clumps of old-fashioned *Iris pallida* that came from a single crowded clump near the old front porch (I had to move them before demolition). Adding to these basics, I've sowed blue flax, desert bluebells, and Indian blanket, as well as (free) divisions of creeping phlox, thyme, snow-in-summer, and other bits and pieces from friends. With their donations, coupled with plenty of digging and weeding, my hovel is now a home and it's surrounded by a garden. Let me show you around.

Making Things Grow

When I was a young gardener, one of my favorite books was *Making Things Grow* by Thalassa Cruso. An Englishwoman transplanted to America, she wrote in a no-nonsense style, exactly the opposite of what I expected from a Brit. She became a frequent guest on the *Tonight Show* with Johnny Carson and she would become exasperated by his fumbling when repotting houseplants or whatever the topic was. I became fascinated by this small, angular woman with a French braid perched on her head. Later on, she penned another book called *To Everything There Is a Season*, in which she wrote of the triumphs

Designing on a budget needn't be dull. The pink-striped blades of New Zealand flax contrast effectively with kale, dahlia, and mum blossoms.

and tribulations in her own garden. My sister loved this book, too, and we joked about our long letters about our gardens back and forth from Colorado to Florida, just the way Thalassa wrote to her brother back in England. One story concerned planting the garden to come into perfect form for her daughter's wedding. Alas, temperatures were below normal that year and it all bloomed brilliantly a month too late. I've never forgotten her candor or the inspiration I got from reading her work. It made me want to become as good a gardener as she. It made me want to know everything about making things grow.

That's exactly the way it turned out. My life revolves around plants, both personally and professionally. Although I love designing (especially if given someone else's extravagant budget), some of my favorite time is spent planting seeds, rooting cuttings, and potting up bulbs. I love the feel and smell of the earth, working with the seeds or tubers and imagining how my labor will pay off. Every gardener needs a basic primer on making things grow. Learning about types of plants and how best to propagate them will put you in good stead for every growing situation you face. The details and timing vary a bit depending on where you live, but the basics remain the same. Let's get started.

A Sunless Greenhouse

Many gardeners envy those with greenhouses. With just a little ingenuity and a small investment, you can turn a sunless room into a greenhouse to start hundreds of plants for your summer garden. A basement, spare room, laundry room, or even a large closet can be converted to support plant life. All you need are inexpensive shop lights that hold fluorescent light bulbs, a humidifier, timer, and some shelves or tables. An old kitchen table or door placed over two sawhorses will do just fine. Hang the shop lights from the ceiling on chains so they can be easily raised or lowered. The ideal height for the lights is just a few inches above the tops of the plants, so being able to raise them is vital as the plants grow. Both the lights and an optional humidifier can be plugged into a timer.

Set the timer to give the plants fourteen to sixteen hours of "sun" each day. Don't worry about keeping the room warm. Sixty-five to 75 degrees is ideal during the day, falling to 50 to 60 at night. Too much heat will promote straggly, over-stretched plants; cooler temperatures encourage compact, husky young plants. Excessively expensive units with sodium vapor lamps can be purchased, but they are equally expensive to operate. They grow amazing plants but aren't cost effective for general gardening and are therefore outside of this discussion.

All About Annuals

Reading seed catalogs is one of my favorite winter pastimes. Many people do this online, of course, but I like hard copy. I narrow down my list of favorite new annuals and vegetables to try, imagining how they'll look in summer. Then I realize I've picked enough varieties to plant my entire neighborhood, so I whittle

I've always been fond of the old-fashioned striped mallow (Althea zebrina)*, a charming annual that often has the knack of sowing itself exactly where it will look lovely, such as among bee-magnet alliums.*

down my list again. I also check out what's new on the seed racks at the garden centers. By midwinter there's a wicker basket on my kitchen table stuffed with packets of seeds.

Most seed packets will tell you when to start each variety of seed indoors. Most should be sown six to eight weeks before the last average frost in your area. I start my seeds beginning in mid- to late March, continuing until mid-April for the fast growers. You can also use your greenhouse to start cuttings from plants you may have overwintered from last summer such as coleus and geraniums, but more about that later.

Seed-starting kits are available at nurseries and garden centers. A plastic tray with twelve six-packs is called a flat. You can also buy a clear plastic dome that fits snugly over a flat. This creates a warm, humid environment for seeds to germinate. Fill the six-packs with a sterile potting soil (the best choice is a soil mix formulated for seed starting), sow the seeds, water from the bottom to avoid washing the seeds away (I always water from the bottom even after the or three seeds in each cell. After they germinate, I thin them back to one per cell. Sometimes I gently transplant the unwanted seedlings, using a little pickle fork, into new flats.

You'll be amazed how many plants you can grow in a small space. In midspring, you can begin to move your flats of plants outside. Put them in the shade at first, gradually exposing them to more sun each day. It takes about a week to complete the hardening-off process. Take them indoors

Like confetti after a parade, moss roses litter my garden path.

seeds have sprouted), cover with the dome, and place the flat under lights. A heat mat helps speed germination. It's somewhat like an electric blanket that is placed under the flat and removed when the seedlings sprout.

Practice makes perfect. If you're new to growing plants from seed, and since conditions vary, you may want to try a few batches ahead of time. Try lettuce or spinach. Once the seeds germinate, feed them with a water-soluble fertilizer each week and check them daily to make sure they stay evenly moist. I usually sow two

Not for Pots

These annuals are best sown directly in the ground for several reasons. Some grow so quickly there's no big advantage to starting them early; they often get leggy. Some transplant poorly and may either die or never be as vigorous as those sown directly in the ground.

Bachelor's buttons
Beans
Beets
California poppies
Corn
Dill
Forget-me-not
Kale
Larkspur
Lettuce
Love-in-a-mist
Mexican sunflowers
Morning glories
Mustard
Nasturtium
Peas
Radishes
Shirley, corn, and bread seed poppies
Spinach
Sunflowers

Sow seeds of bread seed poppies in fall or midwinter; after the first year they'll form colonies.

if night temperatures drop below 50 to 55 degrees.

The best candidates for starting inside include peppers, eggplant, tomatoes, marigolds, impatiens, ageratum, balsam, flowering tobacco, coleus, zinnias, and salvias. They will greatly benefit from the indoor head start. You may be tempted to go wild and start all your seed indoors, but many varieties are best sown directly in the ground at the appropriate time. As early as midwinter in the South and Southwest, and around St. Patrick's Day across much of the rest of the nation, you can sow peas, sweet peas, larkspur, California poppies, bachelor buttons, Shirley poppies, lettuce, and spinach. Wait until after the last frost to sow sunflowers, cosmos, nasturtium, corn, beans, and morning glories. They grow so quickly in warm weather that they'll quickly catch up to comparable seedlings started indoors.

Striking Cuttings

One skill every gardener needs is the ability to strike cuttings. At very moderate expense, you can start new plants from the cuttings of existing plants. The best candidates for this include tropical perennials and shrubs that we grow as summer annuals outside, such as geraniums, fuchsias, flowering maples, begonias, hibiscus, coleus, and lantana. It's also possible to take cuttings of hardy perennials and shrubs in spring and early summer. These include lavender, santolina, thyme, creeping veronica, vinca, and many others.

All you need is a sunless greenhouse or perhaps just a bright windowsill, plastic pots and tray, sterile potting soil, a small artist's brush, clear plastic bags, rubber bands, short bamboo stakes, and a rooting hormone available at your local garden center.

For most plants, the cuttings you take should be from 3 to 6 inches in length with at least three pairs of leaves. Make the cut about ½-inch below a pair of leaves. Strip off all the leaves that will be below the soil surface when the stem is inserted in the pot. Roots will form along the stem where the leaves used to be (called the leaf axils).

*Notice that I've thinned the seedlings of maroon bread seed poppies
and orange California poppies so that the plants have enough room to develop fully.*

*In my zone 5 garden, I grow oleanders in pots
and winter them on my sun porch.
New plants can be made from cuttings.*

~

*Hibiscus add tropical beauty to my patio.
They, too, may be propagated
from cuttings.*

Dust this area lightly with the rooting hormone, using a small artist's brush dipped in the powder. The powder also contains antibacterial and antifungal agents to help prevent rot and disease.

You will probably want to reuse last year's plastic pots; be sure to run them through the dishwasher first. You threw them away? No worries—just use cottage cheese containers with holes punched in the bottoms for drainage. (You can also use egg cartons instead of plastic six-packs.) Fill the pots with sterile potting soil and let them stand in a tray of tepid water for several hours before inserting the cuttings. When the soil has soaked up the water and is evenly moist, drain any remaining standing water in the tray.

Candidates for Cuttings

African mallow

Angel's trumpets

Angel wing begonias
such as 'Red Dragon'

Blue potato tree

Cape fuchsia (Tecomaria)

Cape plumbago

Flowering maple

Fuchsia

Geranium, including scented,
ivy-leafed, and fancy-leafed

Hibiscus

Ivy

Licorice plant

Marguerite daisy

Oleander

Purple heart

Salvia

Sweet potato vine

Vinca

Wandering Jew

Make holes in the soil with a pencil and carefully insert the cuttings; firm the soil around them.

Use short bamboo stakes in each pot to hold up a clear plastic bag that you'll cover each pot with. Secure with a rubber band at the pot rim and you have a minigreenhouse. In this steamy environment, the cuttings may root within just a few weeks. You can check to see if they have rooted by giving the cuttings a very gentle tug. If they resist your tug, the cutting has "struck." You can then remove the plastic tent.

The two conditions to monitor closely are overwatering and hot sun. You will probably need to water only once initially until the cutting strikes since there will be very little evaporation under the plastic

Geraniums and coleus such as 'Kong Rose' are among the easiest of plants with which to practice your skill at striking cuttings.

~

This particular specimen of 'Red Dragon' begonia is three years old and nearly the size of a Volkswagen. I've started dozens of new plants from its cuttings.

Starting life in a plastic pot in my bedroom window in March, this startling 'Red Futurity' canna moved out to the balcony with the warm weather.

I store dahlia tubers, such as those of 'Blue Angel', in the basement in winter, reactivating them in March. Pinching the growing tips promotes better branching and blooms.

tent. Never let the pots stand in water since this may cause rot. A very sunny window may be too hot for the cuttings under plastic, so make sure your area doesn't heat up too much on a warm day. The morning sun of an east-facing window may yield the best results.

Starting Summer Bulbs

When the first bulbs and perennials have barely burst into bloom in early spring, it's already time to plant summer-flowering bulbs. Some of the most spectacular plants for beds and containers, summer-flowering bulbs include hardy ones such

as lilies and tender bulbs such as dahlias, cannas, begonias, oxalis, gladiolus, and elephant's ears.

Shop in late winter to get the best selection. Garden centers stock tantalizing arrays that, in their dormant state, are relatively affordable. Lilies may be had for as little as a dollar a bulb, while cannas and dahlias generally cost about double that. (If you wait until they're growing in gallon pots, the price will at least quadruple.) Bulbs are best stored in a cool, dark place until you plant them; early spring is the right time to start many of them indoors across the northern half of the country. While gladiolus and oxalis can sit tight until midspring, you can achieve spectacular results if you plant many others about a month before the last frost, giving them a head start on the growing season.

Lily bulbs may be planted directly in the ground or in large pots outside. They need time to put their roots down. If left inside their plastic bags, lilies will sprout and become contorted stems trying to find an exit from their imprisonment. Lilies grow best in loose, sandy soil. If you have clay soil, you'll get best results by planting them in large pots or patio planters where you can give them the soil they prefer. Plant them 6 to 8 inches deep. Squirrels like lily bulbs, so you may want to place some chicken wire over the soil until they sprout. And if they emerge from the soil in April and frost still threatens, simply dump some extra potting soil over them for protection.

If you saved dahlias, cannas, begonias, and elephant's ears last fall, they're likely already sprouting by late winter. I place mine in plastic supermarket bags, loosely tied, and store them in complete darkness in the basement. Other gardeners prefer crates filled with dampened peat moss. By March, the bulbs have had enough of their winter dormancy and are ready to go. Some bulbs have already started to form twisted masses of rhizomes (horizontal stems from which roots and shoots emerge). To deal with this, for example, I wrestle canna rhizomes apart with the help of pruners to make small clumps with two or three growing points, usually called "eyes." Repot in fresh soil in gallon

Cannas such as variegated 'Pretoria' grow quickly in the heat; this shot was taken a month after a hailstorm had stripped it of all but a single leaf.

plastic pots and place them in a sunny window or sunroom. A trick with dahlia tubers is to plant them in pots only half-filled with soil. As they sprout and grow, add more soil until they reach the top. This will result in strong stems with good root systems. When the stems are about 6 inches tall, pinch out the growing tip (usually the top ½ inch) to encourage them to branch out.

Elephants in the Garden

Perhaps the biggest leaves you can grow in your garden—here or almost anywhere in the world—belong to elephant's ear.

A potted jungle of blue potato tree, 'Red Dragon' begonia, yellow oleander, dahlias, geraniums and yellow cape fuchsia (Phygelius) *obscure the garden beyond, which Mouse heads out to explore. (Yes, I have a cat named Mouse.)*

Native to tropical Asia, elephant's ear (species of *Alocasia* and *Colocasia*) can grow to an astounding 2 feet or more in the shape of, well . . . elephant's ears. In Hawaii the tubers are harvested, boiled, and mashed to make the culinary dish poi. Don't try this at home. The tubers need expert handling because they contain irritant crystals that can scrape and swell the tongue and throat.

It's the leaves of the plant, however, that whet our gardening appetites. Bright emerald green and jaw-dropping in size, the plants reach their peaks in the heat of summer. Some selected varieties such as 'Black Magic' have very dark foliage, while others, such as 'Illustris', are green with purple-black stems and leaf veining.

To get your elephant's ears going, buy and plant them in midspring. Use plastic pots big enough to accommodate them comfortably (plenty of room for the root system). Keep them moist and warm and the tubers will sprout in a few weeks. Keep them in a sunny window until mid- to late May, then transfer them to a very large pot in sun or part shade. A glazed, resin, or plastic pot may work best since it will hold moisture better than a terra-cotta pot. Water and feed regularly, protect from wind gusts, and you may have the biggest plants in the neighborhood. Unlike most plants, elephant's ear likes wet feet and is often used as an accent in ponds. These eye-catching plants can be effectively combined with coleus, sweet potato vine, and other tropical plants that also enjoy moist soil. Elephant's ears used to be a popular feature of many gardens in the Victorian era as well as in the fifties and sixties. Perhaps it's time for them to take a place of prominence again.

More Bulbs and Tubers

Tuberous begonias differ in their needs from almost all other bulbous plants. They can be started in a shallow tray of soil with the depressed side of the tuber up, just barely covered with soil. Transfer them to larger, quart-size pots as they grow. Ultimately they'll find their final homes in hanging baskets and larger pots where they receive filtered summer sun. The "nonstop" varieties, available in a rainbow of colors, have proved to be the absolute best that I've grown over the past twenty-five years.

Dahlias and cannas also make great container plants, once again reveling in loose, nutritious soil. Dahlias make superb cut flowers so are ideal for growing in the vegetable garden, where they'll benefit from regular moisture and staking to support their brittle stems. Smaller types make great patio plants. The tubers look like small, thin potatoes attached to a central stem. Use a gallon plastic pot, then cover the tuber shallowly with soil. As it grows, add more soil. It will root along the stem, making a sturdier, more vigorous plant. When the plant is about 5 inches tall, pinch out the growing tip to encourage it to branch. Do this again from the new stems when they're a few inches long. The result will be a compact, bushy plant with lots of

Elephant's ears in my garden don't achieve the mammoth proportions they attain in more humid climates. Still, they're impressive amidst begonias, salvias, purple heart, and fancy-leaf geraniums.

flowers. Transplant outdoors either into pots or into the ground once night temperatures stay reliably above 50 degrees. Dahlias do best when kept slightly moist at all times and given regular feeding every few weeks.

Cannas also benefit from a head start inside. Once again, plant the rhizomes in pots big enough for them. It depends on

Persian buttercups (Ranunculus) revel in temperatures from about 35 to 60 degrees, along with pansies, coral bells, and spring bulbs. They fizzle when summer heat arrives.

their size but generally a gallon pot is fine. They start slowly but rev up when the mercury climbs. Plant them outside the same time as dahlias and fertilize liberally to promote the growth of luxurious leaves and flowers. Cannas are always best the second season and beyond when they've grown to their full stature. First year rhizomes only hint at their beauty, bulking up in the coming years.

An exotic summer-flowering bulb for the adventurous gardener is the gloriosa lily. Native to India, this is a twining vine that needs support, lots of water, fertilizer, and heat. The plant's amazing red and yellow flowers have a spidery, exotic look. Start it in midspring in a gallon pot, laying the long tubers on their side

covered by about an inch of soil. Provide a bamboo stake for the vine, eventually transferring the entire plant into a large pot with ample support in late spring. With a bit of fussing and feeding, the flowers of this tropical beauty will astound you in summer.

As I write this in late April, the French doors in my bedroom are open to the warm spring sunshine. On the west-facing balcony are flats and flats of this year's crop of summer bulbs, mostly dahlias, cannas, and elephant's ears. When the sun sets each day, I shuttle them indoors to sit with tropical plants that have been overwintering inside—things such as cactus, succulents, palms, Cape plumbago, and a passionflower

Like many of my plants, this passionflower vine winters indoors and vacations in summer on my balcony, growing luxuriantly and flowering exotically.

vine. At this time of the year, my bedroom is more jungle than sleeping quarters. I'm looking forward to that magic day when it's safe for everything to go outside for the summer and I'll have my bedroom all to myself. This scene is repeated throughout the house—wherever there are sunny windows. If you become a mad patio gardener like me, consider the consequences.

More Beauty from Bulbs

Many smaller or lesser-known bulbs can provide great interest for a small price. Some are suitable only for certain regions of the country, but many grow and flower over a broad range of conditions. Gladiolus top the list. Easy, dependable, and inex-

pensive (sometimes priced as low as ten for a dollar), gladiolus grow almost everywhere and come in a staggering array of colors, many with contrasting shades in the interiors of the flowers. I can't think of a color not found in their ranks. Some of the bicolor combinations are downright surreal.

Plant the papery corms with an unusual metallic sheen about 5 inches deep in a sunny spot. Many people put them in rows in their vegetable or cutting gardens for ease of culture since the big hybrids need staking to keep the stems from snapping. Keep planting from midspring through early summer, every week or so, to ensure waves of flowers for cutting. Gladiolus are really best for cutting since they look awkward and stilted in a perennial garden. Because these lovely flowers have long been abused in dreadful flower arrangements in which they're splayed out in geometric fan shapes, they've gotten a reputation as somewhat tacky flowers. The arrangements certainly are; the flowers are not. When I had back surgery many years ago, some friends who knew my aversion to those horrid arrangements, brought an enormous arrangement of hundreds of gladiolus. It was the size of a Volkswagen. I asked the nurses to put it at their recep-

Inexpensive and easy, Abyssinian gladiolus possess grace, beauty, and a fragrance reminiscent of talcum powder. Dig the corms in fall and store in mesh bags.

tion desk, saying innocently, "So that everyone can enjoy it."

To my mind, gladiolus are best displayed casually, plunked without arranging into a big crock or vase. If you still can't get too many funeral arrangements of gladiolus out of your head, you might prefer the smaller nanus or butterfly types that grow to about half the size of the standard types. All gladiolus are native to the Middle East and Africa, particularly South Africa, and the modern hybrids have all been developed from wild species. In the South in early spring, many gardeners grow the perennial species *Gladiolus byzantinus*, a pretty thing with magenta flowers. Californians often grow the lovely *G. tristis*, an elegant early spring bloomer with fragrant cream-colored blossoms brushed with yellow and beige. So-called Abyssinian gladiolus (*Acidanthera murielae*) is closely related and is one of my favorites. The plants grow to about 2 feet tall and look like regular gladiolus until they bloom with loose sprays of lovely white flowers with maroon markings in the center. Their sweet fragrance is a bonus. Like *G. byzantinus* and *G. tristis*, Abyssinian gladiolus fit easily into any garden setting.

Other small African bulbs include highly fragrant freesias, purple baboon flower (*Babiana*), tubular *Watsonia*, and *Ixia*. All of these when in flower are best as winter and spring accents in West Coast gardens, although if you have a sunroom or greenhouse they can be enjoyed anywhere during early spring. Montbretia, pineapple lilies, lily-of-the-Nile, and oxalis, however, can be grown in summer almost

*I'm crazy about South African pineapple lilies (*Eucomis*) displayed with an actual variegated pineapple plant, pink bougainvillea, and the ever-present offspring of 'Red Dragon' begonia.*

everywhere. Montbretia come in vivid vermilion, orange, yellow, and gold, with sprays of small, tubular flowers above foliage like that of gladiolus. They're hardy up to about zone 7; in colder climes they need to be dug and stored like gladiolus.

Pineapple lilies have always struck me as one of the most endearing bulbs. A thick flowering stem emerges from a rosette of leaves. The stem is studded with small, star-shaped flowers of either pale chartreuse or wine red, with a tuft of leaves at the top. The effect is somewhat like a pineapple, albeit a skinny one, and a pot of them is charming. They're in bloom for a long time in summer—up to two months—and multiply each year.

Lily-of-the-Nile (*Agapanthus*) originated far from the Nile. Once again, this is a bulbous plant from South Africa, a region that is a treasure trove of wonderful plants, containing about a tenth of all the species on the planet. Tubular blue agapanthus flowers top tall, leafless stalks above short basal leaves. I sometimes envy Californians, who drive past these beautiful flowers that are so easy to grow that they colonize highway median strips. Though the 'Headbourne' hybrids are reputedly hardy as far north as zone 6, bringing these flowers within reach of more gardeners outside the West Coast, most cold-winter gardeners need to grow them in pots. The shorter 'Peter Pan', just a foot tall, makes a small statement on my summer patio.

Oxalis, sometimes called wood sorrel, often fool people into thinking they're shamrocks because retailers sell potted specimens by the millions on St. Patrick's Day. They do have foliage like four-leaf clovers, but they bear no relation to the Irish clover. Their flowers are small and pink or white, but leaves are the reason for growing oxalis. The variety 'Iron Cross' has dark maroon blotches on the inner parts of the four green leaflets, while the leaves of 'Purpurea' are a solid, dusky eggplant color with contrasting pale pink flowers. Both varieties are attractive when planted to spill out of containers or tucked around ground covers and shorter annuals in the garden. Plant the tiny corms in midspring, pushing them just a few inches into the soil.

Peruvian daffodils (*Hymenocallis*) resemble spring daffodils but bloom in early summer. In white or pale yellow, these sweetly scented flowers grow from bulbs and have strap-like leaves that are wider than those of real daffodils. Because they are tender in all but frost-free regions, Peruvian daffodils grow best in pots. When fall arrives, bring them indoors, reduce watering, let the foliage die back, and reactivate them in spring.

When fall comes to cold-winter areas, allow the gladiolus, Abyssinian gladiolus, pineapple lilies, montbretia, and oxalis to frost. Dig them up, cut off the foliage, and spread them on newspaper for a few days to dry. Then stuff them into plastic netted bags such as the ones oranges or onions come in at the supermarket. You can also use old nylon stockings for this purpose. Place an identification tag, listing color and species, in the bag with them to avoid confusion and unwanted surprises next season.

Agapanthus are best brought inside before they frost and overwintered in a sunny window, sunroom, or greenhouse. Cannas can also be moved in before frost and treated similarly. They stop flowering and gradually look completely disheveled, but I've found that once moved outside the following summer, they grow like gangbusters—they grow thicker and are faster to bloom than cannas that sat in plastic bags in the basement through the winter. Space restrictions will dictate how you treat them.

On the Cool Side

Some bulbous plants are best suited for the coolest of weather—as long as it doesn't freeze. Anemones, Persian buttercups, and paperwhites (*Narcissus tazetta*) have an unorthodox comfort range between 35 and 65 degrees. In parts of the South, California, and the Pacific Northwest, gardeners can enjoy them in their gardens in late winter and early spring, while high-altitude gardeners can grow them in early summer after the last frost. For most of the country, these tender spring beauties are for spring display as long as they can be protected from frost. Inexpensive bulbs, they need some practice to get right for individual conditions. In frost-free areas they can be planted in the ground or in pots, while everywhere else they're strictly for pots. Plant them in fall in the South, California, and the Pacific Northwest, or in winter indoors.

The 'De Caen' anemones bear the name of the region of France where they were first selected from wild species and popularized as florist's flowers. With lustrous, shiny petals in sensuous colors of

Learning the secrets of plant parenthood helps to populate your perennial garden. I rely on easy, no-fuss flowers such as salvia, catmint, white cranesbill, penstemon, and snow daisy.

pink, purple, and violet, they have a riveting black center. Cool, damp conditions suit this variety perfectly. The same goes for Persian buttercups (*Ranunculus*), another stunning flower with hundreds of overlapping petals like the tissue paper flowers you see in Mexico. I especially value them on my spring patio, displayed with tulips and daffodils, where their vivid colors of red, yellow, orange, wine purple, and white are quite exciting. I constantly watch the weather forecasts in case I need to pull them into the garage when the mercury drops to freezing or below.

It took me a summer to remove the sad lawn in front of my house and replant it with perennials. Three years later, they bloom with abandon. Even the old garage has found new life as a summer room.

Perennial Parenthood

The easiest way to populate your garden is through division. Not all perennials can be divided, but a good many can. In either spring or early fall, use your digging fork or spade to lift a vigorous clump of daylilies, yarrow, ornamental grasses, or what have you. Depending on its size, you can cut the clump in half or in fourths by thrusting a flat spade through the root-ball. By the way, when you do this wear sensible shoes, as sneakers won't support the base of your foot adequately. Alternately, you can cut through a root-ball with a sharp chef's knife. I've sometimes longed for a chain saw when tackling dense root-balls of ironweed (*Vernonia noveboracensis*) (ironroot is more like it) and some ornamental grasses.

When you divide, cut back the foliage by at least half as you replant. The roots have a good deal of work ahead of them in getting reestablished, and they have a tough time supporting a lot of top growth. Dig a generous hole for the transplant, work in a handful of superphosphate or a slow-release fertilizer. Firm soil around the plant well, build a dike around it to catch water, and puddle it in. Keep quite moist for several weeks and then ease off on the watering as the roots exert themselves.

Many perennials can be grown easily and inexpensively from seed. Some will gladly do this for you right in your own garden without your knowledge or permission. Consider using a bare area to sow perennial seed in either fall or early spring, just the way you'd sow lettuce or radishes. Fall is the preferred season for most perennials since the seeds need stratification—a fancy way of saying they need the alternating freezes and thaws of winters to force germination. Some gardeners prefer a more controlled way of

Catmint and salvia may be increased by division but they're also generous with their seedlings if you forget to deadhead them.

Perennials—To Divide or Not to Divide

EASY-TO-DIVIDE PERENNIALS	PERENNIALS THAT SHOULDN'T BE DIVIDED
Agapanthus	Blue flax
Anthemis	Clematis
Aster	Columbine
Bergenia	Coral bell
Catmint	Delphinium
Chrysanthemum	Feverfew
Cranesbill	Hollyhock
Daylily	Jupiter's beard or red valerian
Hen and chicks	Many penstemons
Hosta	Meadow rue
Ice plant	Monkshood
Iris	Snow daisy
Lamb's ears	Tree peony
Lamium, lamiastrum	
Lily turf	**PERENNIALS AND SHRUBS TO PROPAGATE THROUGH CUTTINGS**
Monarda	
Oregano	
Oriental poppy	
Ornamental grasses	Clematis
Phlox	Lavender
Rhubarb	Potentilla
Rudbeckia	Rockrose
Salvia	Sage
Sedum	Santolina
Shasta daisy	Shrub roses
Yarrow	Sunrose
	Thyme

planting, sowing the seeds in fall in pots, layering them thinly with coarse sand or very fine gravel to prevent them washing away, and storing the pots on a north side of a house all winter. Consider placing them in plastic crates to keep them from tipping over. The seeds germinate in spring, and then they can be pricked out individually into tuna quarters. They usually reach sufficient size (if you've nurtured them lovingly) to plant out in late summer or early fall. Don't wait too long: they need their roots to be firmly established before facing the rigors of winter.

Chapter Two

Season to Season

*T*iming is everything in gardening. What happens in your
garden often needs to be planned
and executed up to three seasons
in advance. For example, spring-
flowering bulbs need to be planted
in fall. And the glories of the late-
summer garden, cannas and dahlias,
need to be potted up in late winter.
When money is no object, a person
who doesn't plan ahead can simply
buy what's in bloom. For the rest of
us, it's all about doing what's
needed at the proper time. It's hard
to keep up.

Winter in Miami or San Diego is
quite different from one in Denver
or Des Moines. What follows are
only general guidelines to help you

I spend the winter dreaming of and planning for the summer.
Most of my patio plants are saved from year-to-year such as the large angel's trumpets tree,
or grown from cuttings such as coleus and geraniums.

plan. I've lived in the South and the North, and, though we need to make allowances for weather differences, gardening is amazingly similar across much of the country. Again, the trick is to work out the timing.

WINTER

Early Winter
- pot up bulbs for forcing
- protect vulnerable plants outside
- order seed and nursery catalogs
- begin winter watering
  as needed
- compost leaves and
  garden debris

Midwinter
- clean and oil tools
- start garden cleanup
- compost
- start feeding indoor plants again
- order seeds and bulbs
  from catalogs
- groom indoor plants; take cuttings
- winter watering as needed
- move forced bulbs to windowsills
  for color
- take antidepressants

Gardeners' New Year's Resolutions

The depth of winter is always a tough time for gardeners. We've still got several months before we can get back to doing what we love, but we can resolve to do it better. We can even begin right now.

Order seed and nursery catalogs.
You can pick up a gardening magazine to find offers for catalogs. You can discover new varieties and familiarize yourself with them and—most importantly—you can plan and dream for spring.

Resolve to grow more from seed.
You'll not only save money by doing this, but you'll also extend your planting options far beyond what you can find in six-packs this spring.

Feed the birds.
If you want feathered friends to take care of insects in the garden, provide food, water, and shelter all year long. They'll repay you in many ways.

Start a compost pile.
You can go about this in a casual manner, starting with eggshells, coffee grounds, and old lettuce from your kitchen. You'll be surprised how quickly your kitchen and garden debris turns into nutritious compost that you can add to potted plants and vegetable patches. Avoid citrus and grass clippings, and you'll have an odor-free pile.

Resolve to avoid pesticides.
Your garden can be healthier and more self-sustaining if you use only natural remedies for pests. In general, let the birds and "good bugs" like ladybugs and spiders take care of aphids and white-flies.

Do more with less water.
Don't let water restrictions ruin your garden. Reduce turf areas and plant more drought-tolerant perennials and shrubs. A water-thrifty garden can be just as lush

and romantic as one that guzzles water like a thirsty horse.

Find some great windowsill plants for your great indoors.

Be adventurous. Pot up some amaryllis or try your hand at African violets, orchids, or cactus and succulents. You'll make your home more beautiful and you'll stay happier this winter.

A Touch of the Tropics

Many people take houseplants for granted. But they do far more than merely fill an empty corner. Plants take up pollutants—notably carbon dioxide—and release oxygen. This trait is especially valuable during winter when our homes are closed up tightly.

The majority of our houseplants are very adaptable, low-maintenance plants with iron constitutions. They can put up with drafts, low light, and low humidity. Most are native to tropical and subtropical areas around the world; those most tolerant of low light levels grow beneath rain forest trees so they have no problem surviving in our dim living rooms.

Most small specimens of houseplants are quite affordable. With patience, a small collection can grow into an indoor jungle in just a few years. Don't kill them with kindness: let your plants dry out between waterings, fertilize sparingly— especially during winter—and move them into a larger pot only when their growth slows and they appear ready to break out of their current pots.

Winter is one of the best times to start or enhance your collection of tropical indoor plants. If you have east- or north-facing windows, consider ferns, palms, pothos, umbrella tree, philodendron, fig tree, asparagus fern, false aralia, African violets, ivy, and dracaenas. There are many new varieties of foliage houseplants with variegated or golden leaves to break up a green monotony.

With south- or west-facing windows, you can grow an even wider assortment of plants. Any collection can be improved with the addition of supplemental grow lights and a humidifier. For the adventurous gardener, consider bromeliads, miniature pineapples, moth orchids, camellias, jasmine, gardenia, azalea, dwarf citrus trees, bird-of-paradise, and angel wing begonias.

Help for Horrid Houseplants

Although winter can be a good time to add plants to your indoor collection, it can also be a tough time for houseplants. Days are short, the sun's rays are at their weakest, and humidity levels plummet due to dry furnace heat. To compound matters, some gardeners both water and fertilize too much, causing such problems as root rot, fungus, gnats, and weak, straggling growth.

Most of our classic houseplants (excluding winter bloomers such as orchids and African violets) should be treated with benign neglect during winter. Keep watering and fertilizing to a minimum, with just enough of each to keep the plants healthy. They are simply in a "holding pattern," where they grow slowly if at all. Most plants benefit from a slowdown period, rather than receiving a constant barrage of stimulants.

As spring approaches, however, the longer days encourage new growth. All of my houseplants vacation outside in summer. To get them in shape, I'm evaluating and treating any problems that have occurred over their winter confinement. Some will need pruning, some get haircuts, and others may need division and repotting.

Potted trees such as ficus, citrus, blue potato tree, avocado, and angel's trumpets should be pruned for shape. Take out dead branches and branches that are too close together. If the tree has been in the same pot for several years, consider repotting. At the least, scrape off the top few inches of soil and top-dress with fresh potting soil. Resume fertilizing every few weeks, with the most liberal feeding from April to August. You can use either a water-soluble food that you apply as you water, or slow-release pellets that feed all summer. I do both. (I usually cut down on fertilizing in late summer in preparation for bringing the plants back inside.)

Some bushy plants may have lost their compact shapes and become tall and gangly. Things such as umbrella plants, geraniums, rubber plants, rosemary, fuchsias, and lavender can be re-shaped now. Cut off the weak, straggly growth to create a pleasing mound shape. Sprawling and vining plants probably need a radical haircut to rejuvenate them. Ivy, wandering Jew, purple heart, grape ivy, pothos, philodendron, bougainvillea, and asparagus fern all benefit from a cutback. However, if the plants are still looking full and graceful, resist the urge to trim. Cuttings may be rooted to create new plants if you desire.

I added a little sun porch to the west side of my house for my tropicals in winter and to keep me somewhat sane.

Once again, start an aggressive watering and fertilization program.

When plants appear to have become too cramped for their quarters, it's time to repot. Select a new pot just one or two sizes larger, avoiding going from a very small pot to a very big one. The danger in this is in accidentally creating a soggy mass of soil that leads to root rot. Some plants can be divided as you repot, such as mother-in-law's tongue, wandering Jew, aloe, and agave. The first two should be knocked out of their pots and cut in half with a sharp knife, then repotted. The latter two should be removed and then the offsets, called "pups," gently teased away. The mother plant should go into a new, larger pot with fresh soil, while the pups should go into very small pots that suit their sizes.

Orchids for Sweethearts

A bouquet quickly fades and a box of chocolate disappears as fast, but orchids remain a perpetual token of affection. Growing orchids isn't as daunting as some people might think and most can be accommodated quite easily in almost any home. The number-one indoor plant in the country, orchids attract just as many men as women, making them a great gift for any sweetheart.

With 30,000 species known throughout the world, orchids are found in every continent except Antarctica. Many hybrids swell that number to astronomical heights, making orchid-growing an exciting hobby that can last a lifetime. Most orchids that are commercially available are relatively easy to grow. In addition, they thrive at temperatures that are comfortable to us in our homes, with the ideal being 70 to 85 degrees by day and 50 to 65 degrees at night. All you need is a bright windowsill, with an east or south exposure being the best. Too much light will turn the leaves yellow-green, whereas too little light may be indicated by very dark green foliage. If your orchid isn't flowering, increase the light levels (supplemental lights may help) and fertilize with a fertilizer formulated for orchids, such as Dyna-Gro 3-12-6.

Because of their diversity, you can have orchids in bloom at any time of the year. Many of the most popular kinds flower in winter and early spring, making them especially rewarding for the home orchid fancier. In addition, the individual flowers of most orchids are exceedingly long lasting, with some lasting up to an incredible six months. Orchids don't actually need much water but should be kept relatively moist while they are setting bud and blooming. Because most orchids grow in the wild on the trunks and branches of trees, wrapping their roots tightly to the bark, they are grown in a bark-based growing medium. Wetting the roots well is the key to keeping your orchid plants healthy; never let them stand in water. In the Deep South, many gardeners attach their orchids to their trees with fishing line; soon after, they will cling to the bark by themselves.

Increased humidity can achieve good results. You can group the plants in trays on the windowsill with gravel in the bottom to collect excess moisture as it drains through the growing medium. As this water evaporates, the plants will benefit from the increased humidity. A humidifier can also be helpful during dry winter months, along with a fan to help circulate the air. Keep the plants away from the hot, drying blasts of a heat register.

A Gardener's Checklist for Late Winter

Late Winter
- plant seeds inside
- pot up summer-flowering bulbs

Pleione orchids (ABOVE) and lady slipper orchids (RIGHT) prove to be much easier to grow than they look.

DENDROBIUM ORCHIDS are among the most varied of the classifications, with flowers in many colors and in almost limitless variety. Wild species are native to Australia, the Pacific islands, and much of Asia. Many of the flowers are fragrant and very long lasting, making them very popular.

CATTLEYA ORCHIDS are often used for corsages, making them the most recognizable of all the orchids. With exquisite fragrant flowers, these so-called catts vary from pure white to yellow, lavender, purple, and even red. They are native from Mexico to South America. Some flowers are very small and charming, while others may be as large as a dinner plate.

MOTH ORCHIDS (*Phalaenopsis*) are some of the most popular and easy-to-grow. White, pink, mauve, and wine-red colors predominate. Native to tropical Asia, they can flower at any time of year, but are most floriferous in late winter and spring. A spray of flowers may last up to six months depending on your conditions.

LADY SLIPPER ORCHIDS (*Paphiopedilum*) are also found in tropical Asia and into the Himalayas. They are noted for a large pouch that resembles a lady's slipper (well, perhaps in bygone days) and deep, rich colors such as maroon and purple. Because the plants stay compact, they're great for cool windowsills and the flowers stay fresh for several months.

PANSY ORCHIDS (*Miltonia*) mimic the garden flower with their shape and the distinctive "waterfall" of color in the center of each blossom. Found in Central and South America, pansy orchids are compact, sweetly fragrant, and easy to grow on the windowsill, with flowers appearing mainly in spring.

VANDA ORCHIDS like more sun than most other varieties and originated in tropical Asia. With many bright, dazzling colors, vandas vary widely in size from miniatures just a few inches tall to plants that can reach several feet in height. The flowers may last several months.

ONCIDIUM ORCHIDS grow throughout the Americas and have become some of the most popular of all. Exotic in their flower shapes, markings, and colors, oncidiums have graceful sprays of long-lasting, often highly fragrant flowers. They produce more and more flowers each year and usually flower several times a year.

PLEIONE is a small genus of orchids native to southern and eastern Asia, found mainly in cool, moist mountainous areas. Though these plants are considered miniatures, their flowers are relatively large and very pretty. The central tube of the flower, called the labellum, is strongly fringed and its interior often heavily spotted. Colors range from hot pink to blends of cream and pink to white.

- spade vegetable garden
- scatter annual seeds such as larkspur, poppies
- finish garden cleanup, compost
- prune
- divide and transplant perennials
- pull cool-season weeds
- consult last year's photos to plan revisions and additions
- plan layout of vegetable garden
- prepare beds for planting by digging and adding organic matter
- start tomatoes, peppers, and squash indoors
- sow cool-season vegetables such as peas and spinach directly in the ground
- delay sowing corn and beans until soil warms and frost danger has passed

Premature spring fever hits in epidemic proportions in late winter. Gardeners need to channel their energies wisely to perform the tasks that most need to be accomplished at this time. Take it slowly, stretching and using muscles that often haven't been put to much use over the winter.

The most important task at hand is to finish cutting back perennials and ornamental grasses. The old foliage has protected the crowns of the plants all winter. Now it's time to remove it to allow room and sunshine for new growth. Cut as far down as you can on the old stems to reveal it. Put the old, dried stems in the compost pile if you have one. If you don't, simply start a pile with this debris. Don't worry about raking up every stray leaf and twig since small, crumbly bits will be worked into the soil by earthworms. It's best to cut down and clean up when the soil is dry. Wet soil compacts easily and when you step around the plant, your weight will squeeze necessary oxygen out of the soil. Many perennials are already showing new growth, as we might expect this time of year, with crocus, snowdrops, and daffodils budding and blooming in warm, sunny spots. Clear away debris from emerging bulb foliage.

Get going in your vegetable garden. The frost is out of the ground and it can be easily spaded or tilled while it's relatively dry. This is all in preparation for the first phase of planting. Cool-season crops can usually be safely planted around the middle of March, with St. Patrick's Day being the traditional time for planting peas and sweet peas (earlier in the South and on the West Coast). They revel in the very cool days of late winter and will fail to develop properly if sown later when it's too warm. The timing varies widely, depending on your latitude and altitude, and even from year to year. The "absolutes" we used to read in gardening books often no longer apply as our weather has become less predictable. You can also plant out starts, seedlings, and seeds of onions, strawberries, beets, radish, mustard, spinach, lettuce, and other greens. These also grow well and taste best when they develop in cool temperatures. A lightweight row cover (available at garden centers) keeps these crops from getting too cold at night, but they can take a light frost.

Believe it or not, late winter is also an ideal time to get the jump on weeds. I usually go after the cool-season culprits such as dandelions, shepherd's purse, wild oats, and clover. It's also easy to spot bluegrass that may have infiltrated your beds and borders. Get after it now before it spreads.

If you potted up spring-blooming bulbs and stored them in a dark garage, shed, or crawlspace last fall, many will be ready to bring into bloom now. You can grow them on a windowsill or on your patio. Cover them or bring them in if nights drop much below 20 to 25 degrees. If you didn't force any bulbs last fall, you can pick some up at your nursery. Daffodils, tulips, crocus, and hyacinths are just the right tonic for the gardener with spring fever. Combine them in a basket or bowl with primroses and other seasonal plants for a lovely display or gift.

Vegetables

Most people in our country don't grow their own vegetables. That's too bad. Pulling beets or carrots from the earth or plucking vine-ripened tomatoes or peppers are some of the great rewards of gardening, perhaps even more satisfying than raising pretty flowers. For me, it depends when I last ate.

I've always loved to work in the soil, something I learned at an early age in my parents' extensive vegetable garden. I can't recall any vegetables we didn't grow. As a result, there was no fussing about eating vegetables at the dinner table, even the notoriously unpopular spinach, okra, squash, broccoli, and brussels sprouts.

They do taste better fresh from the garden (before the sugars break down and turn to starch). Also, the personal investment of sowing, weeding, and watering somehow increases their sweetness.

Homegrown produce is the healthiest. While a few heat-loving crops aren't particularly suited for areas with cool summer temperatures, such as at high altitudes, most everybody can grow great vegetables. Even people who garden on balconies and rooftops can harvest delicious salad greens, root crops such as beets and carrots, as well as vining vegetables such as cucumbers and squash. The key is to select compact, bush-form varieties if you're gardening in a small space. There are even varieties of tomatoes that produce prolifically in a hanging basket.

Gardeners complain about their soil more than almost anything else. One of the keys to getting good results in your garden is to understand the nature of your soil and what it's capable of growing. Don't assume that any kind of soil is "bad" and automatically needs to be "improved." Your soil may be well suited to some kinds of plants but not to others. Vegetables are in the high-maintenance group that requires that super-duper soil that nobody seems to actually have.

A loose, friable soil—something like potting soil—is the standard to work toward. Don't laugh. In just a season or two, you can help create a perfectly good growing medium for vegetables wherever you garden. As you plan for planting— especially if you're a new homeowner— try this simple test with your soil. When the ground thaws, pick up a small amount of soil and try to roll it into a ball. If it falls apart, you've got sandy soil. If it rolls into a mud ball, you've got clay. Don't worry, you're not alone; the majority of gardeners across the country seem to have clay soil. Though it can be difficult to work, clay soil retains moisture well (an advantage in times of drought) and is mineral rich. Sandy soil, on the other hand, drains very quickly, requiring more irrigation. Neither has a significant amount of the organic matter that is vital for good results with specific types of plants such as vegetables and many annuals and perennials.

The plants best suited to clay soil are often native wildflowers and adaptable plants from regions around the world that have similar soils. You can avoid much aggravation and disappointment by planting what wants to grow in your soil rather than types that are doomed to failure. For vegetables, of course, it's possible to amend your soil to support them better. That's where manure comes in. Manure-based compost—especially from cows and sheep—is the preferred way to modify both clay and sandy soil to get better performance from vegetables and many traditional flowers such as roses and lilies. (Manure isn't good for native wildflowers that have evolved with a lean, mineral-rich, low humus soil; though it can often benefit woodland wildflowers and ferns that evolved in humus-rich ground.)

If you wish to amend parts of your yard for a vegetable or rose garden, start in late winter or early spring as soon as the soil can be worked. Spread several inches of manure-based compost on the soil and till or dig it in. Add more each year, including

your own compost derived from garden debris and kitchen vegetable scraps.

If you use fresh manure, make sure that it is well rotted before you incorporate it. It takes several months in the open air for this to happen (you can tell when it's ready to use when the odor becomes negligible). Fresh manure is very high in both ammonia and nitrogen and will burn or even kill plants.

You will find that manure, when used properly, helps produce high vegetable yields and bigger, more floriferous perennials and roses. Farmers have been taking advantage of manure for thousands of years. So don't just turn your nose up at manure—it can be a gardener's best friend.

With relatively little effort, you can make your soil more productive for growing crops each year. I cover my vegetable plot with leaves each fall. To keep them from blowing away, I toss on more loose garden debris, including the contents from plant containers after the first killing frost. In spring, after the soil has thawed, I add more manure or compost and it's an afternoon's work to fork this all into the soil.

If your soil is excessively rocky or claylike, you may wish to create raised beds to which you can add a mixture of topsoil, compost, and manure for an ideal growing medium. (We'll talk more about raised beds in Chapter 4.) Big pots and half whiskey barrels can also be employed to grow vegetables; just make sure to provide holes for adequate drainage.

Growing vegetables is easier than you might think. If you start with workable soil and follow the directions on seed packets about planting depths and sowing times, your chances of success are good. Regular, even moisture is also required for best results. Before you plant, plan how you'll irrigate your crops. Some people like drip systems or soaker hoses, while others prefer the convenience of overhead sprinklers. I actually water by hand because of the series of very shallow "canals" that traverse my vegetable garden. I just fill the canals with water and let it soak in. The only exception is for tomatoes. Each of these plants lives in a shallow basin surrounded by a dike of soil to hold water, whether from the sky or the hose. The tomatoes stay evenly moist with this method.

But I'm getting ahead of myself, since in late winter we're most concerned with planting. Give the soil a good, even spading to about 8 or 10 inches, then rake to smooth it and remove rocks and clods. If you prefer the canal method of watering, you can create them with a hoe. Don't get hung up on creating perfectly straight rows, since sometimes crops are best grown in squares or blocks. For example, I often form a grid with the hoe to make square-foot planting areas to plant the shortest, most compact vegetables such as radish, beets, spinach, turnips and lettuce. My garden looks like an inverted waffle. Native peoples of the Southwest relied on this waffle-style arrangement to conserve moisture in their gardens and the technique is still practiced today. In rainy regions, rows of crops are raised above ground level to keep the roots from rotting. It's all about adapting to the characteristics of your region.

It's vitally important to sow cool-season crops in late winter, even earlier in the South. You can plant seeds or transplant young seedlings of lettuce, spinach, peas, beets, radishes, and onions. They can withstand a light frost—even snow—and develop rapidly during cool, sunny weather. Warm soil is essential for beans, corn, and squash to germinate well. A caution: one unseasonably hot day doesn't mean it's safe to plant. Wait for temperatures to stay reliably above 50 degrees at night before sowing them. This also applies to transplanting peppers, eggplant, and tomatoes.

SPRING

Early Spring
- continue potting up summer bulbs indoors
- continue seeding, indoors and out
- continue garden clean-up, pruning
- set out frost-hardy annuals
- bring out forced bulbs for patio display
- start patio containers
- clean ponds, pumps, filters
- update spring gardening wardrobe

The Lowdown on Lilies

Millions of Easter lilies are purchased and displayed each year. Not many survive for more than a week or two, after which they go out to the dumpster with the foil candy wrappers and Easter basket grass. Is there a way to prolong the life of an Easter lily in your garden? The answer isn't yes or no, but maybe—depending on your individual conditions. Before we get to the details, let me remind you that there are many beautiful lilies that can grace your garden, and now is the appropriate time to plant them (unless you accomplished that task last fall).

Many species of lilies are found throughout the northern hemisphere, including North America. While many flowers are often labeled lilies, such as daylilies, canna lilies, and peace lilies, true lilies are distinguished by several characteristics. Their bulbs are composed of scales, making them resemble artichokes, and the flowers are borne on straight stems with many short leaves. This differs from daylilies, for example, which have long, grassy leaves and leafless flower stems.

Almost all of the true lilies we grow in our gardens are hybrids derived from species native to Asia. The Easter lily, scientifically called *Lilium longiflorum*, is native to subtropical Asia, making its survival in colder parts of the country a bit difficult. If you'd like to try to grow yours in the garden, find a sunny position near the foundation of your house. Wait until mid-May in zone 6 northward (keeping it watered in a bright window in the meantime), then plant it about 5 inches deeper than it's currently growing in its pot. This may help to keep the bulb from freezing in winter. If the stems emerge next spring before May—as they are apt to do during a premature spring warm-up— and a freeze is forecast, simply dump some potting soil over them. This trick works well for a lily or any other plant that jumps the gun and is tempted to emerge too early for its own good.

There are other factors that can also affect how lilies fare in your garden. The easiest way to kill a lily is to plant it in clay soil, in shade, under a downspout. Do the opposite and give your lilies sandy loam soil, sun, and regular moisture with good drainage. If your soil isn't suitable, grow lilies in raised beds, planters, or large pots. Lilies make excellent container plants and add pizzazz to your patio in summer.

Garden centers offer many types of hardy lily bulbs that can be safely planted in the ground or containers right now, with best results if you accomplish this by mid-April. There are three main groups of lily hybrids. Asiatic hybrids are often the first to bloom, usually in June. Noted for their many bright colors, they can range from 2 to 5 feet in height and are tough and dependable, even for mountain gardeners. Though lovely, they lack fragrance. The classic tiger lily with orange flowers and black spots is related to this group of lilies and figures in the parentage of many hybrids. Unfortunately, almost all tiger lilies carry a virus that doesn't affect them but is fatal to other lilies. Chewing or sucking insects such as aphids can easily spread it. If you grow tiger lilies, you may have to be content with them alone since they are the "Typhoid Marys" of the lily world.

Trumpet lilies are amazingly fragrant. Their huge, trumpet-shaped flowers, usually on tall stems 4 to 6 feet in height, distinguish them. Gold, yellow, white, pink, and plum are the main colors. Trumpet lilies bloom in midsummer. Some of the most popular varieties include 'Pink Perfection', golden orange 'African Queen', purple 'Midnight', and 'Golden Splendor'.

It's easy to become a lily fanatic. June-blooming 'Sunny Twinkles' is an Asiatic hybrid that's easy to please in large pots or well-drained garden soil.

Oriental lilies delight us with their large, exotic, intensely perfumed blooms. They come in shades of pink, red, white, and yellow, often with contrasting bands of colors and spots. They usually range from 2 to 5 feet in height. Perhaps the most famous of this group—and one of the most popular cut flowers in the world—is 'Stargazer', a tough, dependable lily with rosy red petals with white margins freckled in deep red. I grow these in very large pots that I leave out all winter. They come back faithfully each year, growing to about 2 feet tall, with flowers that scent the entire neighborhood in late July and August. Unlike other lilies, Orientals can benefit from being grown in partial shade. This makes them good candidates for balcony gardeners who may not have completely sunny conditions. Other popular Oriental hybrids include white 'Casa Blanca', white and yellow 'Garden Party', and lavender pink 'Sorbonne'.

Within the past decade or so, the range of hybrids has grown by quantum leaps. Hybridists have managed to make crosses between groups that were previously thought impossible. Trumpets have been crossed with Orientals (called Orienpets), Asiatics with trumpets and—most astoundingly—Easter lilies with Asiatics. One of the first of these amazing hybrids is called 'Triumphator'. With the classic Easter lily funnel shape, it is white with a pink throat, carries a sweet fragrance, and is perfectly hardy. So even if you don't manage to make a go of it with saving your potted Easter lily, you can plant 'Triumphator' and plan an Easter egg hunt in July.

Most lily bulbs are grown commercially in the Netherlands. If you become a lily fanatic (it's hard not to), you may wish to check out the catalogs of the premier growers and hybridizers in our country.

Vines

Vines are opportunistic plants. They have evolved to rely on other plants with sturdier structures to support themselves.

The Orienpet hybrid lilies (crosses between Oriental and trumpet lilies) have it all—substance, fragrance, and exotic loveliness.

Through grasping, weaving, and twining they elevate themselves to a place in the sun. It's no wonder that our common speech includes negative connotations toward vines. We talk about "social climbers" and needy "clinging vines." In some cases we view vines with suspicion, fearing that ivy will dislodge mortar between bricks or that wisteria will systematically disassemble our houses. These fears are lodged in both truth and myth. Kudzu vine indeed "eats" barns in the South with frightening speed, and what child can forget Sleeping Beauty's castle being engulfed by impenetrable rose briars?

We shouldn't be afraid of most vines (although I tremble at the thought of a hardy form of kudzu). They can make graceful, colorful additions to our gardens, garlanding structures and cloaking fences and walls. Each one has its merits. If only every chain-link fence in the nation were planted with sweet peas or clematis, this would be an even better place to live. There's a great example in my neighborhood where climbing red roses have been patiently twined through every square inch of an otherwise utilitarian fence. The result is stunning. The owners get privacy while passersby get a visual feast.

Some vines, such as annual morning glories and sweet peas, are well equipped for climbing, while others such as clematis are really just perennials with posture problems. Clematis are deservedly popular for their lovely flowers but they need help, especially at the beginning. They can't cling to walls at all and need to be coaxed and tied onto trellises and other structures. As they mature, clematis weave more strands into themselves (like a hair weave), finally becoming more self-reliant. Have patience with them the first few seasons.

For faster results, plant sweet peas or morning glories. They require patience only at germination. You will need to nick the seeds with a nail file or rub them in sandpaper to break the hard seed coat. I do it the easy way, soaking them in tepid water overnight before planting them directly in the ground. The window of opportunity to plant sweet peas is a small one, usually accomplished about St. Patrick's Day across the northern tier of states, and as early as January in the South. Sweet peas (*Lathyrus odoratus*) are native to southern Italy and Sicily and thrive in cool temperatures. Plant in a trench supplemented with compost, and provide ample water and support for the vines. With an extensive color range, sweet peas bloom prolifically if kept picked. Their sweet, spicy fragrance has made them favorites for generations.

Morning glories should be sown in the ground when the danger of frost has passed. They may start slowly but make up for it when the heat's on. Don't make the mistake that a friend of mine did last year. Frustrated by their slow growth, he fertilized the plants extravagantly, resulting in tropical growth that would make a kudzu proud, but no flowers. Morning glories perform well almost everywhere and can be breathtaking at their peak. My favorite is the classic variety 'Heavenly Blue', but new varieties are now coming into the seed market, thanks largely to Japanese breeders. A friend gave me a packet of a red variety with a segmented flower instead of the traditional funnel shape. It's called 'Split Personality'. My friend told me he spotted it on the seed rack at the store and immediately thought of me. Hmmm . . .

Not every gardener is a fan of morning glories. They self-sow all too rampantly in many parts of the country and may grow as rapidly as kudzu. I pull a couple hundred unwanted seedlings from beneath the arches in my vegetable garden each spring. Still, they're mighty pretty, so you may wish to enjoy them in an isolated spot such as on a fence next to the driveway or in an island bed surrounded by lawn. The seedlings that may sprout in the lawn will be no match for a lawnmower.

Another vigorous grower that may be slow to flower is wisteria. There are some issues with this perennial vine, beloved for its graceful dripping sprays of lavender pea-like flowers in May. One is that it can take a very long time to bloom. My advice is to save up and buy a specimen that is in bloom this spring at the garden center (proving that it will bloom at an early age). Also provide wisteria with an extremely sturdy support; it will reduce lesser supports to splinters with its muscular twining trunks. Think "anaconda" as you build the support.

There are other great vines that don't have the floral flash but that can be useful and attractive. Grapes, porcelain vine, silver lace vine, Virginia creeper, Englemann ivy, and Boston ivy quickly form dense canopies of leaves that can create a wonderful shady haven. The ivies turn crimson and mahogany in fall. Friends who have burgeoning plants will surely let you take cuttings, which are relatively easy to root in spring. A new variety of silver lace called 'Golden Lace' features chartreuse foliage. I planted tiny tuna quarter pots on trellises next to my patio to provide a bit more privacy from the street. I'm confident. Perhaps you need a similar screen. If your patio or deck faces west or south and is uninhabitable on hot days, consider constructing a sturdy frame over it. Plant some vines and reclaim your patio.

Midspring

- spread topdressing
- prune roses, feed
- prune spring-flowering shrubs after they finish, evergreens as necessary
- divide and transplant perennials as needed
- fertilize spring-flowering bulbs
- plant lilies, gladiolus
- plant hardened-off perennials
- buy new tropicals
- take allergy medication

Early Patio Color

Most patios are bare this time of year. Not mine. It's packed with early spring potted plants that flourish in the cool temperatures of spring and can even shrug off a light frost. If your patio or balcony seems bare and lifeless—devoid of color—pot up some early spring bloomers and foliage plants that will make you feel that spring has truly arrived.

Is your patio bare in spring? Pot up tulips and daffodils in fall, chill them and bring them out
in March and April. Add Persian buttercups, stock, pinks, pansies, and coral bells.

A full, lush summer look starts with winter planning. Thyme, red dianthus, and purple verbena carpet the soil with lamb's ear; blue fescue grass and catmint are set farther back.

Pansies, stock, and cape daisies bloom prolifically with weekly feedings in spring.
Potted plants can be covered or whisked inside if a blizzard threatens.

The advantage of potted flowers is that if the weather takes a serious turn for the worst, they can be whisked inside easily. I'm not about to whisk a hundred pots inside just because of some snow or light frost. Most of the plants I'm enjoying can take all but a hard freeze, generally 25 degrees or less. The most vulnerable I will remove from harm's way on a really chilly evening.

The perfect plants for spring pots include cold-tolerant annuals, bulbs, and early perennials. They can be combined to produce dazzling displays now, rather than waiting for late May until it's "safe" to plant out traditional container plants. The plants I'm describing below also make

great container plants for gardeners at high elevations, though it's still too early to contemplate putting most of them outdoors, except perhaps for the pansies.

Among the cold-tolerant annuals that delight us now are ever-popular pansies, bright annual dianthus (*Dianthus chinensis*), English daisy, dusty miller, and spicily scented stock. Forget-me-nots are an old-fashioned favorite, with sprays of tiny blue or pink flowers. Iceland poppies glow when the sun hits their crinkled petals in colors such as pink, orange, peach, yellow, and white, as luminous as a stained-glass window. Pretty pink, coral, or lavender twinspur (*Diascia*) can survive a touch of frost, as can glowing sun or cape daisies

A living tapestry of sedums, verbena, and Corsican violets
beats a boring expanse of bark mulch any day.

(*Osteospermum*) in vibrant shades of orange, melon, yellow, pink, purple, and violet.

The most glorious of the cool-season flowers is the Persian buttercup (*Ranunculus*). Above parsleylike leaves, it carries flowers up to 5 inches across and composed of hundreds of petals, as if they were made from tissue paper. Persian buttercups come in many pretty shades such as white, yellow, orange, red, pink, and plum.

All of these annuals look perfectly at home with hardy spring bulbs. If you potted them last fall and forced them in your garage or basement, they're probably coming into bloom now. If you didn't, garden centers did it for you and you can enjoy tulips, daffodils, and hyacinths now. After they've flowered, you can plant them in the garden to bloom again next spring.

Early, frost-tolerant perennials add immensely to a spring display. And, for balcony gardeners with fairly shady conditions, these can be featured throughout the summer. These include hostas, with beautiful broad leaves, but make sure to keep them safe from frost and the burning, afternoon sun (not to mention hail).

April Action

A gardener in spring needs to be part wedding planner, part caregiver, and part workhorse. There are so many details to juggle, so many plants that need attention, and so much physical labor. People who don't garden may think that gardeners stroll around in straw bonnets snipping roses to a Vivaldi soundtrack. Not me—I sweat. Buckets. I usually lose about twenty pounds between April and July, coming tantalizingly close to fitting into those 30-inch waist Levis that have languished in my closet for a decade. Maybe this summer, I tell myself. That's a good enough reason to garden even if I didn't like plants.

I live for the growing season, which starts earlier and ends later than most people think. Many people get a burst of horticultural enthusiasm about the middle of May. They fight the crowds at the nursery, buy one of everything that's in bloom, plunk these plants in unprepared soil, swaddle them in bark mulch, sit back and wait for a miracle. It doesn't come.

Here's the problem: many of the plants they buy may be inappropriate for their climate and their particular growing conditions. Many will have been pushed into bloom ahead of schedule, trucked in from California and Texas. The end result is a bunch of unhappy plants, trapped in a sea of bark nuggets, that quickly fizzle and fade.

Don't wait till May to plant pansies if you have hot summers.
Their cute faces are to be enjoyed in the cool months before heat shuts them down.

Try your hand at fantastic spring combinations with Iceland poppies, maroon-leaf coral bells, whirligig Osteospermum, Marguerite daisies, *and variegated acorus.*

An experienced gardener takes a different approach. I start formulating my plans in winter, ordering seeds and summer bulbs. The garden gets a good cleanup and cutback during the warmest days of March, while the vegetable patch gets spaded and raked. I usually plant peas, onions, and salad greens around St. Patrick's Day. In April, I begin to sow warm-season vegetables and annuals inside, things such as tomatoes, peppers, eggplant, flowering tobacco, zinnias, and marigolds. There are really two phases to spring planting, with cool-season flowers and vegetables commanding my attention outside now, and the warm-season tropical plants taking over in mid- to late May. Success is all in the details, dependent on knowing what needs to be done at the proper time.

Trouble is, we work with weather, something that has enormous mood swings: one day it's kissing the garden with sunshine and showers, and the next it's slapping plants with a hard freeze. I'm constantly shuffling flats of tender plants inside and out again, gradually exposing them to more and more sun, but keeping them inside at night when temperatures drop below 50 degrees.

During April, my energy is focused on several projects. This is an excellent time to plant and transplant perennials. It's much less stressful to them now when sunshine is abundant, but temperatures remain cool. If the perennials you buy at your favorite garden center have been hardened off properly, you can plant them at anytime. I'm not talking about greenhouse-grown delphiniums in their full glory that wind and frost will demolish in no time.

The best values are plants grown in smaller pots—usually tuna quarter and quart size—that will give a respectable show this summer and catch up to gallon-size plants by next season. Steel yourself to buy plants that aren't yet in bloom. Read the tags to determine the months they bloom for a succession of flowers through summer and fall. Otherwise you'll end up with a garden that blooms early and sputters in summer.

As you shop, look for ground-hugging spreading perennials to serve as living, blooming mulch. Ice plants, thyme, sedum, dianthus, and creeping veronica cover the soil far more beautifully than bark ever could. Ground-cover plants shade the soil to conserve moisture and grow and bloom in concert with taller perennials and shrubs planted behind them. Contrary to popular opinion, mulching with bark is not good for your plants. Not only does it look horrible (don't take your design cues from fast-food restaurant plantings), but, as microorganisms break down the wood, they steal the nitrogen from your plants. Heavily mulched beds of plants never put on much growth and will sit in suspended animation almost indefinitely.

People have been brainwashed into thinking that mulching with bark is a good, "natural" thing. There's nothing natural about it: there's no ecosystem on the planet where trees shed their bark and uniformly spread it on the ground. Forgo the bark mulch and instead lavish some nutritious compost on your plants, and carpet your soil with rewarding ground-cover perennials.

Another of my April projects is potting up tropical plants for my summer patio. Every available windowsill is crowded with pots of freshly planted cannas and dahlias. They get a jump on summer since I won't bring them outside until mid- to late May. Even if you can't plant them inside now for lack of space, shop now for best selection and store them in a cool, dark place until May. I'm looking forward to designing my personal patio jungle,

My "explosion in a paint factory" style features maroon and yellow Persian buttercups and orange and magenta cape daisies.

with hundreds of pots of tropical plants, but that's a topic for later.

Allergies

Nature has devised ingenious ways for plants to reproduce. Unlike animals that can roam around looking for mates, plants are stuck where they root. They rely on pollinators to come to them, transferring pollen from flower to flower to form seeds that will reproduce their species. Flowers have evolved in many shapes, sizes, colors, and scents to attract

My garden is much like a living patchwork quilt with the pots of dwarf Alberta spruce bringing a slight sense of order. Note how the California poppies have colonized.

insects and birds. The pollinator gets a reward for stopping by (nectar or pollen), and the flower gets a transfer of pollen to fertilize it. Bees, beetles, butterflies, moths, hummingbirds, and even flies play a part in floral reproduction.

Some flora can't be bothered to put on a great show for the neighborhood fauna. They would rather cast their fates to the wind. This includes most trees (with the exception of fruit trees), grasses, and many weeds. Their flowers are inconspicuous but produce massive quantities of pollen, light enough to be scattered by the wind. Show me a plant with an inconspicuous flower, and I'll show you one that allergy sufferers hate.

To my aggravation, commercials for allergy medications inevitably show garden flowers, implying that they are the cause of your sneezing and watery eyes. Almost all of the flowers we cherish in our gardens, from roses and lilies to poppies and asters, rely on insect pollinators. Their pollen is quite heavy (by pollen standards). They can't just have it blowing away with the slightest breeze. They need it to be ready for their visitors, and it's often sticky so it will cling to some part of the bee or beetle. It doesn't just float around and it's not likely to get in your nasal passages unless you voluntarily bury your nose in a fragrant flower.

If you're a cautious sort, you can garden without fear if you grow flowers with little or no pollen. Hybrid plants that have been bred to have more and more petals in their flowers have pretty much given up on reproduction. Even the most determined bee is frustrated to find pollen

Great foliage plants—lamb's ear, blue fescue, hens and chicks—are the basis for all good gardens.

on flowers that are considered "doubles." Many hybrid roses, marigolds, zinnias, dahlias, and even petunias have tight, concentric rows of petals with little or no pollen. Their pollen-bearing anthers, if any, may become apparent as the flower opens fully, so you can avoid this by deadheading as the flowers pass their prime.

Another aspect of allergies concerns insects. I'm blessed with a taste that mosquitoes find unpalatable, but I'm allergic to beestings. I can't even recall the last time I was stung. I figure the bees

Most of us stop to smell the roses, but have you paid attention to the sweetness of daffodils and the musky scent of grape hyacinths?

know who's rolled out the red carpet for them and they leave me alone. If bees frighten you, try putting a sprig of feverfew in your hat or buttonhole. A pretty medicinal herb from the Mediterranean region, feverfew (*Tanacetum parthenium*) produces small white daisies that bees and other insects avoid. Perhaps they dislike the marigold-like smell. Feverfew is easy to grow in sun or partial shade. A short-lived perennial, it blooms in early summer and again later if promptly sheared back after flowering. It's a pretty addition to any border and well worth the space if it provides peace of mind while you garden.

Fragrance

Mine isn't the ideal climate for a fragrance garden. Two factors work against me: high altitude and low humidity. Fragrance doesn't hang on thin, dry air.

Nonetheless, scent plays an important role in our gardens no matter where we live. It can range from the sweet and exotic to the bracing and refreshing.

Flowers exude their perfumes at different times of day. Some smell most powerful in the midday sun, while others wait until the sun dips below the horizon. There's nothing capricious about it. Flowers have evolved to attract their pollinators when the insects or animals are most active. Sweet alyssum, the humble Mediterranean annual with masses of tiny white, lavender-purple, or rosy mauve flowers, seems to be at its best in the heat of the day. What bee could resist that delicious scent of honey and almonds? Evening primrose (*Oenothera odorata*) opens its sweet yellow flowers at dusk, capturing the attention of tired gardeners and passing moths.

Most of my olfactory encounters in the garden have to be one-on-one. Because the scent of many flowers dissipates in the dry air, I need to get into direct contact. I'm constantly sticking my nose into blossoms as I work in the garden, usually checking for bees before I do so. The big fragrance producers—Oriental and trumpet lilies, old-fashioned roses, and honeysuckle—flaunt their perfumes. They don't need me to champion them for their fragrance. Other plants might not be so noted for their fragrances, especially if they're low to the ground. I spend a lot of time on my hands and knees, deadheading and weeding, so I tend to notice these low growers up close.

Many spring bulbs have delightful scents. Daffodils are softly sweet, while tulips have a dusky tone that's difficult to describe. Grape hyacinths also exude a musky, grapelike odor, while hyacinths top them all with an intoxicating, spicy sweetness. Few early perennials have much scent to speak of—perhaps their bright colors are enough—but there are exceptions. Pinks (*Dianthus*) produce small flowers, with clovelike scents similar to those of their carnation cousins. Some species were called sops-in-wine in England where they were steeped in alcoholic beverages to add their distinctive taste.

Catmint (*Nepeta × faassenii*) is related to the feline delight catnip but doesn't hold much of an attraction for cats. I highly recommend it as a mounding, long-blooming perennial with an almost nonstop display (just now starting) of small lavender-blue flowers. Its gray-green leaves have a bracing aroma like aftershave lotion.

Bearded iris complement their beauty with a very pleasant fragrance when you check them out up close. I'm especially fond of the unusual scent of the old-fashioned pale purple *Iris pallida*, often found in old gardens and alleys, which reminds me of grape bubblegum. When I started my new garden, the only flower on the property was a cramped clump of these old favorites trapped in a narrow strip next to the porch. I divided it into an amazing eighty pieces, planting them in fresh soil throughout my garden. They've grown vigorously in the past two years and as the hundreds of flowers begin to unfurl, I suspect I won't need a close encounter to enjoy the fragrance.

Late Spring
- prune spring-flowering shrubs as necessary
- plant new perennials
- bring out tropicals
- bring out seedlings, summer-flowering bulbs
- buy new tropicals
- seed warm-weather annuals and vegetables from zinnias to gourds
- set out tomatoes, peppers, eggplant
- dig warm-season weeds
- start foxgloves
- take hardwood cuttings
- put out tender aquatic plants
- divide and transplant bearded iris as needed; cut back foliage by half and plant each individual "fan"
- tie tomatoes to sturdy stakes as they grow; try strips of old panty hose.
- help climbers such as beans, morning glories, and clematis with acrylic green yarn.
- deadhead hybrid tea roses as they fade, but don't deadhead shrub roses that set decorative hips
- fertilize appropriately

Caring for Spring Bulbs

Tulips, daffodils, and hyacinths usher in the gardening season. We love them when they bloom, but as their foliage begins to ripen and look ugly, our affection fades. If you want your bulbs to be strong and healthy, capable of putting on a good show next year, take steps now.

Start by deadheading the flowers as they fade. This prevents the plants from wasting energy trying to produce seeds. Feed the leaves at this time as well by spraying a water-soluble fertilizer on the plant or scratching in a granular fertilizer around the base of the foliage. If your plants sustained snow or hail damage during the spring, your best course of action is to remove broken stems but leave as much existing foliage as you can.

The leaves feed the plant and the energy is stored in the underground bulb. The leaves will finish their work over the next six weeks or so. The worst mistake you can make is to interfere with this work. Don't remove the leaves until they yellow, eventually becoming brown and crispy. Certainly don't have a tidiness attack and braid the foliage or fold it up with rubber bands. This will weaken the bulbs and diminish their flowering capacity. If you really can't stand the dying leaves, consider planting perennials around your bulbs that are as tall or taller than they are. Meadow sage, Oriental poppy, snow daisy, and catmint are good candidates for this purpose. As they grow and expand, the leaves of these perennials will help disguise the unsightly bulb foliage.

The so-called minor bulbs are beautiful planted amongst low-growing ground covers. The leaves of crocus, snow iris, Siberian squill, grape hyacinth, and glory-of-the-snow fade away unobtrusively, leaving the ground covers to take over after the bulbs finish.

If you forced bulbs in pots for indoor winter display or for your spring patio, you can plant them in the garden as they finish flowering. Until you get them planted, keep them fed and watered and

The spring-fresh flowers of Mexican evening primrose belie the fact
they're blooming on a hot July day. Shop in spring for flowers that beat the heat.

also deadhead the spent flowers. Plant them 4 or 5 inches deeper than they were growing in their pots. Water well, fertilize, and look forward to an encore performance next spring.

Acclimating Your Plants

The Mother's Day weekend marks one of the busiest times for nurseries and garden centers. It's the equivalent of Christmas for department stores. Many thousands of plants will find homes that weekend. Once you bring them home, however, you need to take steps to ensure your new plants will have a safe, healthy transition from the nursery to your garden.

If you buy plants that are displayed outdoors, such as trees, shrubs, and some perennials, they've already been acclimated to your climate. It's safe to plant them when you get home. If you can't get to it immediately, store them in a sheltered spot protected from wind and afternoon sun and keep them well watered.

Plants that have come directly from a greenhouse need special treatment, especially if they're cold sensitive. Plants inside a greenhouse are protected from most of the sun's damaging rays. Leaves burn as easily as unprotected skin, but there's no sunscreen for foliage and sunburnt leaves can't regenerate. When you bring your plants home, expose them to the sun gradually. The intensity of sunshine varies due to weather and elevation. At high altitudes, it is particularly intense and can easily burn leaves in just a few hours. An exposure beneath deciduous trees is ideal, even if the trees have not yet leafed out fully. The dappled shade cast by tree branches will help the leaves become accustomed to full sunlight over a period of three to six days.

Plants of tropical origin are not only susceptible to leaf scald but also can be damaged by cold night temperatures. Even when it stays above freezing overnight, these plants may be at risk if the mercury drops much below 50 degrees F. Day temperatures are largely irrelevant; a sunny, 70-degree day can easily turn into a chilly 35-degree night. Damage may not be immediately apparent, but the cool temperatures may eventually stunt your plants. It may take them a long time to snap out of it, or they may fail to thrive all summer. Leave your tender tropicals outdoors during the day, but whisk them in at sundown. When you're snug in bed, make sure they enjoy the same comfort.

Plants at risk range from true tropicals such as hibiscus, dahlias, and blue potato tree to favorite vegetables including tomatoes, peppers, and eggplant. Of the annual flowers, impatiens, begonias, and coleus are most vulnerable. Annuals that also can be damaged include marigolds, zinnias, sunflowers, salvias, globe amaranth, sweet potato vine, ageratum, wishbone flower and straw-flower, as well as basil. Take the time to acclimate these flowers and you'll have better results all summer.

The Summer Ahead

I'm impressed by how gardeners are finding ways to do more with less water. In my neighborhood—and all over the

West—people have come to terms with less-than-capacity reservoirs. Even in areas that traditionally expect abundant rainfall, it's not as certain as it used to be. By limiting turf areas and planting native and adaptable perennials, shrubs, and trees, our gardens have become more resilient to periods of low rain. And they're more tolerant to heat, insects, and even hail.

We garden in partnership with nature, and sometimes we get the raw end of the deal. The real start of summer is invigorating, as I spy little green tomatoes on my vines and the early perennials turn over the spotlight to the tough midsummer bloomers such as Indian blanket, wine cup, Mexican evening primrose, lavender, and daylilies. On the patio, heat-loving tropicals—bananas, bougainvillea, sweet potato vine, cannas, coleus, cactus, and succulents—grow and flower with abandon.

The key to a healthy, stress-free perennial garden in summer is to surround each plant with an earthen dam that catches water, whether from the sky or from you. If potted plants chronically dry out while you're at work, move them up to bigger, preferably glazed, pots. Otherwise they'll never make it through the summer and you'll just watch them suffer. Don't stress about plants that wilt in the midday sun. It's a natural shutdown, the way we retreat and take an afternoon nap. If they remain wilted as the sun sets, it's definitely time to grab the watering can.

Mist the undersides of leaves often to provide an inhospitable environment for spider mites. Dispatch both mites and aphids with soapy water. Mark your calendars to feed both container plants and vegetables every seven to ten days. Remember that corn is a grass and therefore benefits from a high-nitrogen diet; whereas tomatoes, peppers, eggplant, and most other vegetables prefer less nitrogen. Otherwise, they'll reward you with jungle-like foliage but very little fruit.

Observe your garden this summer. Watch what does best and get some more. Experiment with new species. And if some flower can't stand the heat, get it out of the garden. You can pass it on to a friend who may offer more congenial conditions or you can harden your heart and consign it to the compost. There are always a hundred new plants to try.

Gardening Beneath Trees

Mature trees add value to our properties and enhance our lives by providing shade and cleansing the air of pollutants. The shade we value them for, however, can make gardening beneath them difficult. Besides low light levels, the area beneath trees may be dry and nearly devoid of nutrients because of the tree roots.

Even in this challenging environment, it's still possible to create a beautiful shade garden. Many perennials are especially adapted to growing in a woodland setting. They are native to parts of the country and places around the world with extensive tree cover. There are no shade plants native to the Great Plains and other plateau and savanna areas (since there were no trees for them to evolve beneath). As the result of westward migrations, trees now grow in cities and towns that have sprung up in these areas in the past couple hundred years. The result is artificial urban forests without native shade plants to grow in shady areas. Gardeners in these originally tree-less regions must rely on "imports" to plant under the trees they've planted.

The intensity of light in your shade garden defines what you can grow successfully. Some trees, such as honey locusts, have tiny leaves that allow sunlight to filter through. Others, such as lindens, create a very dense canopy. Pines and spruce create impenetrable shade that makes growing anything beneath them almost impossible. The placement of buildings also affects light levels. If your property is open to the west or south, you may receive more light beneath trees later in the day than an area where buildings block the afternoon sun.

If the area in which you wish to garden could be characterized as "partial shade," your selection of perennials is quite broad. This is an area that gets bright shade and perhaps several hours of direct morning or afternoon sun. Your shopping list can include many kinds of ferns; hostas (noted for their broad leaves); leathery leaf bergenia, with pink spring flowers; brunnera, with blue flowers like forget-me-nots; Jacob's ladder, also with sky-blue bells; goat's

Coleus thrive in a broad spectrum of light conditions, such as here with afternoon shade. These geraniums, by the way, are the old 'floribunda' type, nearly extinct in cultivation.

My own private jungle makes my patio a sensory paradise. The main attractions include several pots of angel's trumpets (Brugmansia) that become almost intoxicatingly fragrant as the sun sets.

Pots of canna, Cape plumbago, begonia, and rudbeckia nestle beneath an angel's trumpets tree. The flowers of this variety open ivory white and change to a tawny peach as they age.

beard, noted for its tall white flower blooms in midsummer; spotted-leaf pulmonaria; fall-blooming white wood aster; and pink Japanese anemone.

Texture and contrast become much more important in a shade garden, which will never be as colorful as a sunny garden. Low-growing, durable ground covers can be woven between the larger perennials listed above to create a living tapestry. Silver-leafed lamium has two outstanding cultivars, 'White Nancy' and 'Pink Pewter', with white and pink spring flowers, respectively. Vinca forms a dense mat of dark green leaves with Wedgwood blue, white, or plum purple blossoms in spring. Variegated forms of vinca are especially valuable for providing interest all season, long after the flowers fade. Woolly thyme also performs adequately in partial shade and can be planted between paving stones. Irish and Scottish moss are also good for this purpose, as is brass button (*Cotula*), a pleasing ground cover from New Zealand with tiny fernlike leaves and tiny gold button flowers.

Spring-flowering bulbs can also flourish beneath trees, since they emerge and flower before the trees have leafed out. Daffodils, grape hyacinths, Spanish bluebells, Siberian squills, glory-of-the-snow, and crocus do quite well. They look delightful when planted near emerging hostas or poking through ground covers.

For deeper shade, rely on ferns, hostas, vinca, and aggressive ground covers such as sweet woodruff, with white flowers in spring, and bishop's weed, which can be bought as the plain green variety or the variegated form with white-striped leaves. This plant is seemingly intent on world domination and is known to burrow under driveways and sidewalks in search of new territory. Bishop's weed can be effective in tough spots, but make quite sure you can contain it before you plant.

In exceedingly dark areas, my advice is to build a deck or patio beneath the trees and enjoy it as a cool refuge on hot days. You may need to construct a slightly raised wooden deck to avoid damaging the tree roots. Decorate with pots of low-light houseplants such as pothos, peace lily, and philodendron for the summer.

Your Own Private Jungle

Though my perennial borders and vegetable garden demand attention in May, my main focus is on my outdoor living areas. This includes two patios—one in sun and another in shade—and my bedroom balcony. Last summer I even converted my detached garage into a "summer room," with two sets of French doors linking it to the patios. Even on the hottest day, my dogs and I have a comfortable spot to enjoy the color and fragrance of the garden, just steps away. We eat, play, and even nap there in our own private jungle. To say that I like container gardening is an understatement. I'm wild about pots—about 350 at last count, collected over a 20-year period—and I figure whatever I can't grow in the ground, I can almost certainly grow in pots.

I think more people would spend more time truly living outdoors if they created a private potted jungle for themselves. As it is, they seem to come outside only to grill a steak and then go back inside to park themselves in front of TV reruns. If you plant your own oasis, it may become your favorite spot to read, dine, entertain friends (four-legged and otherwise), tap on the laptop, draw, knit, or anything else you love to do.

Many sources will advise you how to put together some pleasant summer pots of annuals: but I'm talking jungle. Go wild. Start with the tropical foliage plants that we consider houseplants, such things as palms, ficus trees, dracaenas, bananas, philodendrons, and ferns, depending on your light levels. My tropical plants move indoors for the winter and some have attained almost unmanageable height and weight, so I've added a dolly to my collection of vital garden tools.

Tropicals become the backdrops for flowers. Recall for a moment a grouping of pots you may have displayed on your patio or deck last summer (and let's hope you grouped; "one here" and "one there" just looks like you could barely be bothered and are merely trying to cover

*Since my patio is in front of my house, this dense screen of potted plants—
cannas, dahlias, orange flowering maple, bronze New Zealand flax, yellow angel's trumpets,
and assorted succulents—insures privacy.*

The view from my bedroom balcony reveals the dense container groupings on my front patio. Contrasting foliage shapes, sizes, and textures provide support for the flowers.

stains). Now imagine how that grouping may have looked with palm fronds and banana leaves arching over your annual flowers. And what about your flowers? Did you stick to the basics or did you branch out to the more exotic? How many people plant a six-pack of marigolds in a halved whiskey barrel and hope for some sort of miracle by frost? If you want pots fit for a magazine cover, use a variety of upright, round, and trailing plants with contrasting textures. Jam them in together tightly and fertilize extravagantly.

I have no intention of ever living in California or Florida, but on my patio I can enjoy many of the flowers I see on visits there. West Coast staples such as lily-of-the-Nile (*Agapanthus*), New Zealand flax (*Phormium*), succulents, and bougainvillea flourish almost everywhere in summer. Southern favorites such as cannas, hibiscus, dahlias, and elephant's ears also grow rampantly if given plenty of water and food. I'm crazy about the bold tropical leaves of elephant's ears and cannas. Variegated cannas such as 'Striped Beauty', 'Tropicanna', and 'Pretoria' make especially striking container subjects with their striped foliage and bright contrasting flowers.

The brilliant flowers of dahlias come in almost every shade except blue, but keep the giant, dinner-plate types in your cutting garden, as they need sturdy staking to keep them upright. Go for shorter varieties (3 feet and under) that are manageable in pots. I'm particularly fond of the bronze leaf varieties, newly available at most garden centers, such as scarlet-flowered 'Bishop of Llandaff', orange 'Bishop of Oxford', hot pink 'Bishop of Canterbury', and yellow 'Bishop of York'. With single rather than double flowers, this series is especially charming, but why they're named for British bishops is a mystery.

Varying the size and texture of leaves and flowers creates an arresting arrangement of plants, so it is important to provide contrasts to these bolder plants: good candidates for this are brilliant salvias, flowering maples, begonias, coleus, zinnias, blue potato tree, and pink African mallow,

as well as trailing plants such as verbenas, licorice vine, lantana, and sweet potato vine. All of these grow vigorously if, once again, they are fertilized and watered liberally. Even old standbys such as petunias, geraniums, and marigolds become more glamorous in such tropical company. I also enjoy the scents and textures of lavender, rosemary, scented geraniums, and other herbs, as well as ornamental grasses.

I've saved my favorite tropical plant for last. Angel's trumpets (*Brugmansia*) are native to South America and eventually grow into small trees. Fortunately, they can be pruned to keep them somewhat inbounds. I own half a dozen of these plants, some with white flowers and

I don't miss having a lawn. A billowing summer display
turns my corner lot into a traffic-stopper.

others with salmon pink and pumpkin gold flowers. The tubular pendant flowers measure about 6 inches in length and exude a delicious perfume at night. A good-sized, well-fed plant can display a hundred flowers at a time. My specimens (four years old and 6 feet tall) live on my sunporch in winter and continue to bloom sporadically throughout the year. At their peak in July, August, and early September, the angel's trumpets transform my humble patio into one of the loveliest spots on earth. With some energy and imagination, you can create a private paradise for yourself.

SUMMER

Early Summer

- fertilize containers, vegetables, new perennials
- tear out and compost cool-season flowers and vegetables
- cut back early perennials, provide a shot of food
- start collecting and storing seed
- weed anything that doesn't belong
- summer chores—watering, composting, grooming, bugs

Midsummer

- cut and dry or freeze herbs
- cut and dry everlasting flowers
- collect and store seed
- groom plants

Summer Grooming

With the plants I grow and the words I write about them, the devil's in the details. Color schemes, contrast, harmony, and sequence of bloom in the garden's design

all work to create a beautiful scene. Without a devotion to detail, you might as well forget the whole thing. I'm blessed (or cursed) with my obsession with details. I can rarely spend more than a few minutes relaxing on my patio before I notice that the fuchsia over there is drooping and the bottom leaves on the sweet potato vines look a bit tattered and while I'm at it, I should probably re-arrange that whole container grouping. I keep a list that I update daily but no matter how many chores get crossed off there are just as many to replace them.

Let's start with the patio. I'm wild about all the great flowers and foliage of the "Tropicalismo" style. As I described earlier, my patios—one in sun, the other in shade—are simply overstuffed with pots of wonderful tropical plants that wouldn't be appropriate for my borders.

A potted jungle needs attention to watering, feeding, and manicuring. Morning is an ideal time to give everything the once-over. I take a plastic bucket with me as I groom the plants on each patio. I remove spent blossoms and tattered or bug-bitten leaves. It takes me less than an hour for a once-over. When you remove spent flowers—commonly called dead-heading—cut or pinch the flowering stem off all the way down to the main part of the plant. Some people just remove the old flower but leave its stem. It looks unfinished. Daisies, cosmos, and coreopsis look especially disheveled if you don't remove the entire flower stem.

I'm really fussy about grooming. My goal is to get picture-perfect results since I'm likely to pull out my camera at any time to document my work. You may have slightly less stringent standards. I enjoy the daily contact with each plant because I can sense when something's going awry in time to correct it. Of course, many gardeners would be perfectly content with several hundred fewer pots than me. Then they can spend more time in their borders.

With its gathering of shrubs, perennials, and annuals flowering in concert, a billowing border is one of the glories of horticulture. And any gardener can achieve this luxurious effect in every climate under almost all conditions. To achieve this, you must select the right plants for your site, as well as carefully plan your border's colors, shapes, and textures. Once those pieces of the puzzle fall into place, it's up to you to help it soar. It's all about grooming. Fussy people often make good gardeners. But it's knowing what to do—and when—that's most important. I used to be the most rigorous deadheader in the world. Then I realized that a great many plants offer such handsome seedpods later in the season that by vigorous deadheading, I was depriving the garden of that phase of their life cycles. In one case, I actually removed the spent blossoms of blackberry lily (*Belamcanda chinensis*), a perennial admired far more for its shiny, onyx-like seeds than for its spotted orange flowers. I didn't make that mistake again, but it's sometimes difficult to know which plants to groom and which ones to leave alone.

Most late-spring and early-summer bloomers should be deadheaded. Iris stems should be cut back to the fans of

Make a note on your late summer calendar this minute to order fall-blooming bulbs. Crocus speciosus *should be planted in September for a pretty display around Halloween.*

leaves, but the foliage shouldn't be touched unless you're transplanting them in June. In that case you fork them up, cut the rhizomes apart into individual fans of leaves, discard old, woody bits of rhizomes, cut the fans back by half, and replant at or just below the soil's surface. The mistake gardeners often make is to hack the fans back whether they're trans-

It takes me about 45 minutes to finish daily grooming on the patio, removing spent flowers and tattered leaves. Watering—if needed— takes another 45.

planting or not. It's rude treatment for such giving plants. Cutting off their solar collectors can do nothing to enhance their bloom next season. And the trimmed fans look alarmingly choppy and abrupt, as if some scythe-wielding maniac is lurking in the bushes.

Many perennials can be cut back rather radically to encourage them to do an encore performance. Meadow sages (*Salvia × superba, S. nemorosa*), catmints (*Nepeta* sp.), blue flax, and lavender can receive a buzz cut and, with a shot of fertilizer, quickly rebloom. While this quick whack is easy and effective, it still leaves an unsettling impression. Instead of cutting the foliage back straight across, try feathering your cut the way a good hair stylist does with a razor. For example, cut a sage that's finished flowering back about by half, cutting each stem individually. Shape the plant into a rounded, bush form as you go, cutting the stems back to just above a pair of leaves. New growth and flowers will sprout at this point. It takes more time and trouble to deadhead in this manner, but the results will be subtle and won't affect the overall look of the border.

Some plants aren't likely to bloom again, so cutting them back is a matter of doing the best you can so as not to draw attention to what you've done, carefully taking back the stems just to the basal foliage. Try to be as inconspicuous as possible when dealing with faded veronicas, tall garden phlox, daylilies, valerian, thalictrums, red-hot pokers, penstemons, and sea kale.

It's up to you whether or not you deadhead everything. I tend to leave the stems of some perennials up for fall and winter interest. Coneflowers, black-eyed Susans, globe thistle, bee balm, German statice, and the horehound family (*Ballotta* and *Marrubium*) consort beautifully in their seediness with ornamental grasses late in the season.

Battle of the Bugs

Summer may be plagued by pests. Most people reach for chemical sprays to wage the battle of the bugs. This can be ex-

Butterflies are the reward for a pesticide-free garden. It's been at least twenty years since I've used chemical sprays on insects, relying instead on a soap spray for control.

pensive and, in the long run, counterproductive to achieving a healthy ecosystem in your garden. The populations of insects and other critters in your garden rise and fall in cycles. Some years may be especially bad for aphids or caterpillars, others worse for voles or mice. It all depends on the severity of the previous winter, whether the spring was hot or cold, wet or dry, and the state of predators that eat pests. Bug numbers may be up if birds are down. Rabbits and rodents may get the upper hand if foxes and coyotes have become less prevalent.

Some might think that the perfect garden is achieved by eliminating every living critter on the premises and, indeed, some people spray, trap, poison, and shoot whatever ventures onto their property. There's a better way.

Let's start with pesticides. You don't need them. I haven't used any chemical pesticides in my gardening for two decades, and none in my present garden,

Grow plants that want to grow in your garden and you'll rarely be bothered by pests. Lamb's ear and blue fescue thrive for me, although grasses are often nibbled in bunny-prone areas.

There's nothing that needs pampering in my garden, with perennial stalwarts and self-sown annuals teeming with vitality.

which is the picture of health. I rely on birds and beneficial insects to keep things in balance. Ladybugs, praying mantis, spiders, and predatory wasps can be a gardener's allies. Eliminate them with harmful sprays and you're on your own. Even the birds won't hang around. When the balance tips and aphids pick on the roses or flea beetles bother the sweet alyssum, I get out the soap spray. It's easy to add a couple of teaspoons of pure liquid soap (such as Dr. Bronner's Magic Soap) to a spray quart bottle, shake, and

shoot. Soap softens the hard exoskeletons of insects and they simply dissolve into a puddle. You must score a direct hit with the soap, meaning you need to get to the undersides of the leaves where insects often congregate. Avoid dishwashing liquid or detergents for this purpose because they may cause a phototoxic reaction on plant leaves and burn them.

Most people have favorite ways of dispatching slugs, usually involving beer. I don't do this any more, since the saucers of dead slugs are just as unattractive as the damage they cause. Place pieces of old hose, about six or eight inches long, beneath the plants slugs bother most. After a night of gluttony on your hostas, they'll crawl into the hose to sleep it off. You simply collect the hose pieces, flush the slugs out into a pail, and set them back in place. Some people use down-turned grapefruit rinds in a similar manner. You'll never achieve total control over slugs, but console yourself with the knowledge that they do play a role in the ecosystem, recycling garden debris. Where some of us clash is on the definition of "debris." Never sprinkle salt on slugs. It may indeed kill them, but the salt can be equally harmful to your plants.

Other night feeders, such as earwigs, can be controlled in a similar way. Place loosely-rolled, moist newspapers beneath the plants that they disfigure. They really have a thing for my dahlias. In the morning, as you retrieve today's paper, throw out yesterday's news and the earwigs hiding within.

A bit of damage on plants has to be acceptable. You can even plant favorite flowers and foliage for butterflies, just

Passé? Sedum spectabile *'Autumn Joy'* isn't exactly breaking news in the gardening world but I love its brick red autumn flowers, complemented by sun-bleached tufts of ponytail grass.

Kitty Carlisle, who adopted me after she spent a week in a neighbor's tree, is a tireless mouser. The fire department couldn't reach her, so I hired a tree-trimming company to rescue her out of the cottonwood.

remembering that before the lovely creatures emerge, they're caterpillars munching on your plants. It seems like a fair trade—a few sprigs of dill for a swallowtail. Indiscriminate spraying will ruin any chances of enjoying these beautiful creatures, not to mention killing off the bees that pollinate your fruit, vegetables, and flowers. If certain plants are continuously attacked, year after year, question why you grow them. If they always look miserable and disfigured, what's the point? I'd suggest that they just aren't appropriate for your climate or conditions.

When it comes to plant-eating animals, the best defense is animals that *eat them*. Your own pets, feline or canine,

may help you in keeping some pests at bay. My six pets (three of each) take their pest-control duties seriously and often present me with their catches on the living room rug. They have yet to bring down a deer, however, and if deer, elk, and moose feast on your garden, you either need bigger pets or at least the illusion of them. Many garden centers in areas where deer or rabbit problems are rampant offer various sprays that smell like predators. You can even get genuine bobcat or coyote urine (don't ask me how they collect it). This is dabbed on cotton balls, inserted in plastic holders, and hung around the perimeter of your property to advertise that someone big and bad has marked this territory. Other gardeners rely on sprays of hot pepper, garlic, or tobacco to discourage garden munching, but that seems pretty tame compared to the urine deterrent. A quart of coyote urine, by the way, sells for about eighteen dollars but goes a long way.

FALL

Early Fall
- check out plant sales
- divide and transplant perennials as needed
- take cuttings
- scatter seeds
- pot up perennial seed outdoors
- order bulbs
- plant new crops of spinach and lettuce; cover when necessary
- plant pansies, dianthus, snapdragons, kale
- take tropicals indoors
- find mud boots, gloves, scarves

Ornamental Grasses

I can only imagine how daunting it must have been for settlers in wagon trains heading west. From the Mississippi onward to the Rockies, they waded through an endless sea of grass. Only cottonwood trees clung tenaciously to the banks of creeks and rivers. The rest of the vegetation, covering what we now call the heartland of the country, was predominately perennial grasses, interspersed with dabs of color from wildflowers.

Only small remnants of virgin grassland remain, once one of the most impressive ecosystems on the planet. Today that vast prairie has become a patchwork of wheat and cornfields, dissected by highways and country roads and punctuated by towns and cities. Passengers flying into Denver International Airport don't pay much attention to the geometric patterns below them, nor do they get a sense of the remaining grandeur of the Great Plains.

When I was a small boy, my family lived in the small town of Genoa in eastern Colorado. Our house was on the very edge of town, with views of grass to the horizon. The world seemed very big to me. The prairie was my playground, and I still have vivid memories of exploring the (then) waist-high grass, finding asters, wild roses, and horned toads. On occasion, my mom would visit her sister in Denver with my brother and me in tow. In those days, you simply caught the bus on the highway near the gas station. While we waited, my mom would hitch us to the phone booth with our belts to keep us from blowing away.

When we moved to Loveland, near Colorado's Front Range, I forgot all about grasses. Soon I became big enough to mow the lawn, the tamed, short version of what we had left behind. Never did I imagine that many years later I'd forgo having a lawn altogether and instead create a garden that includes clumps of wild grasses. In an ironic twist, my current garden resembles my prairie playground rather than the stylish, sophisticated gardens I've studied and emulated most of my life. Go figure.

Only within the past two decades have ornamental grasses become really popular, as we have come to appreciate their beauty and the land where they originated. It

Plants we take pretty much for granted, such as barberry and juniper, vie for our attention in fall. They make great companions for ornamental grasses.

seems fitting that our gardens—at least in a small way—echo the natural landscape. Texture and movement are the primary attributes of grasses. They really come into their full glory in late summer. Beautiful in every season—including winter—grasses deserve a home in every garden. They're suitable for planting in perennial borders, xeriscapes, and containers. Their beautiful textures enhance naturalistic plantings such as around ponds and waterfalls.

Varying in height from just 6 inches to over 6 feet, ornamental grasses also differ in their cultural requirements. Almost all require a sunny location, will tolerate any type of soil, and are drought tolerant once established. The grasses detailed here are clump formers (rather than runners like turf grasses), can be divided to increase your stock, and grow well across much of

the nation. Despite their showy seed heads, which are among their most attractive features, most grasses seed themselves rather sparsely, if at all.

For the most dramatic effects, the maiden grasses can't be beat. Towering above the rest is giant maiden grass (*Miscanthus sinensis* 'Giganteus'), growing 6 to 8 feet tall, with thin blades and panicles of tawny seed heads. Zebra grass (*M. sinensis* 'Zebrinus') grows nearly as tall and displays showy yellow-striped leaves. 'Morning Light' and 'Yaku Jima' are maiden grass cultivars of smaller stature. Both grow to between 3 to 4 feet in height and, with their thin blades, resemble a fountain, enhanced by sprays of seed heads in late summer and fall. All of these hold their good looks through the winter and are finally cut back to the ground in

March or April to start the cycle all over again.

Another tall species is plume grass or hardy pampas grass (*Saccharum ravennae*), capable of growing an astonishing 8 to 12 feet tall with adequate moisture. With its stalks of silvery-white plumes that last into winter, it is especially imposing. Feather reed grass (*Calamagrostis* × *acutifolia*) makes a striking specimen for borders. It stands bolt upright and hits about 3 feet in height with its golden seed heads. Select from 'Karl Forester' or 'Overdam', both German selections of this European native grass. Also in the middle range in height, blue oat grass (*Helictotrichon sempervirens*) features thin, blue-gray foliage topped by buff seed heads to about 3 feet tall. It's great combined with catmint, rue, and silver mullein. Blue oat grass is very drought tolerant, as is a miniature look-alike, blue fescue (*Festuca glauca*.) There are several selections of this low-growing species such as 'Elijah Blue' and 'Boulder Blue', both noted for thin, blue blades the color of a blue spruce tree. The foliage grows from 6 to 12 inches high and is topped in summer with tan seed heads. I like to nestle bronze hen and chicks, dianthus, and other creeping ground covers at its feet.

Ponytail grass (*Stipa tenuissima*), also called Mexican hair grass, has quickly

Saturate your fall garden with color and texture, including asters, mums, and variegated artemisia.

You can grow beautiful kale plants to enhance your fall containers. I plant seedlings in my vegetable garden and transplant them when they're at their peak.

become a favorite, especially in the West, because of its exceptional tolerance to drought. Growing a little over a foot tall, its foliage is very fine and chartreuse green. In fall, it bleaches to platinum blond. With very fine blades, it indeed resembles an unruly mop of hair in need of a scrunchie. Its delicate texture can be used to best advantage with 'Autumn Joy' sedum, ice plant, and other perennials with rounded, fleshy leaves.

Another striking color is found in Japanese blood grass (*Imperata cylindrica* 'Red Baron'), a moisture lover appropriate for pond-side plantings. Its foliage varies from maroon to ruby red and is especially pretty when backlit by the afternoon sun. It can tolerate partial shade. So can northern sea oats (*Chasmanthium latifolium*), a lovely grass with the showiest of seeds, flat as if they'd been pressed, dangling from thin filaments. It is especially great for drying for use in winter arrangements.

Midfall

- plant pansies, snapdragons, dianthus, kale
- enhance patios and porches with pumpkins, gourds, mums, asters
- plant bulbs
- dig and store cannas, dahlias, gladiolus, etc.
- plant containers for winter; make fresh and dried wreaths
- empty nonwinter containers; save soil for next season
- sow cover crops in vegetable garden
- reactivate Christmas cactus, amaryllis
- plant paperwhites, amaryllis, cyclamen

Bulb Basics

Novice gardeners often show up at garden centers in spring wanting to buy the tulips, crocus, and daffodils they've been seeing all over town. They're out of luck. Spring-flowering bulbs, because of their unique life cycles, are shipped, sold, and planted in fall.

Just as the gardening season comes to a close and cold weather threatens to

I barter tomatoes for my neighbor's pumpkins.
Kale and mums complement the autumnal celebration.

chase us inside, we're out there putting our faith in the coming spring. It's a connection from season to season as the dormant bulbs put out roots as soon as we bury them, plumping them up for their spectacular spring show. Spring bulbs—in a quirky evolutionary survival scheme—emerge early to attract and be pollinated by bees. Without much competition, they flower, set seed, soak up the sun to store energy for the next season and promptly go dormant once again. They sit out the heat and drought of summer.

Gardeners want value. Bulbs that persist for many years should be your top priority. The ones that thrive across much of the country—in a wide variety of conditions—include snowdrops, snow crocus, snow iris (*Iris reticulata*), squills, wild species of tulips (as well as some hybrids), grape hyacinth, hyacinth, and most kinds of daffodils.

Ask most anyone where tulips come from and they'll tell you Holland. The image of windmills and tulips has become part of our collective consciousness, the product of a 400-year-old advertising campaign that puts Coca Cola and McDonald's to shame. While the Netherlands grows and ships the vast quantity of bulbs planted each fall around the world (although Washington state's Skagit Valley is hot on their heels), none are actually native to that picturesque country. Tulips, for example, grow wild in central Asia, largely on grassy high plains and

Red 'Apeldoorn' and 'Golden Apeldoorn'
tulips spark my spring groupings.
Both are Darwin hybrids, good bets for
garden longevity as well as forcing in pots.

reclaimed from the sea. Our conditions are quite different. The trick to growing great tulips is to select the ones that retain the survival skills of the wild tulips of central Asia.

Growing wild species can be very rewarding. Not as tall and big as the hybrids, they are still quite pretty and some not only survive but also multiply and thrive as if they were natives. This includes pretty apricot-colored *Tulipa batalinii*, starry yellow and white *T. tarda*, and candy-striped red *T. clusiana*. They have another advantage since their bulbs are much smaller and therefore easier to plant. Other smaller, tough tulips close to the species are hybrids distinguished by interesting mottled leaves and bright blooms. The Kaufmanniana hybrids, such as cream white 'Zombie' and pale yellow 'Waterlily', have graceful, slender buds with outer red petals that open to star-shaped flowers on sunny days. The Greigii hybrids also feature mottled foliage and big flowers on short stems, such as 'Red Riding Hood' and 'Pinocchio', red with broad white edges on the petals.

If you want the classic tall, bright Holland tulips, the best are the Darwin hybrids. Most of us associate Darwin with "survival of the fittest," and these hybrids are quite fit for our gardens. Corvette red 'Apeldoorn' and shiny yellow 'Golden Apeldoorn' are the classics; a few dozen I planted nearly twenty years ago now number in the hundreds. Also recommended are apricot-orange 'Daydream', yellow-edged-red 'American Dream', red-edged-yellow 'World's Favorite', orange 'Lighting Sun', and ivory white 'Maria's

plateaus with clay soil, cold winters, and hot, dry summers. Their natural habitats and climates bear a striking similarity to my own. Millions of tulips have been planted here over the past century. You'd think that, except for the windmills, our country would resemble the colorful fields of Holland each spring. Trouble is, a good "doer" in Holland isn't always a good "doer" here. For more than three centuries, the Dutch have bred and selected bulbs that thrive in their rainy, cool, cloudy climate in the sandy soil they

Dream'. Add to this the "flamed" Darwins, with showy streaks on a plain background such as 'Beau Monde', which is ivory with rose-red flames; 'Olympic Flame', which is golden yellow with crimson flames; and 'World Expression', which is butter yellow with pronounced red flames. In recent years, the 'Impression' series of Darwin hybrids has impressed gardeners everywhere with their beauty and vigor, including 'Pink Impression', 'Red Impression', and 'Salmon Impression'.

If you garden in a region where frost rarely threatens, chances are that tulips and other spring-flowering bulbs won't succeed for you. A cold winter chilling is as important to their life cycle as are the sunny days of spring. Some people go through a refrigeration process—similar to forcing—to enjoy the spring flowers. The bulbs won't return the next season, so just consider them annuals.

Tulips are the most vulnerable of the bulbs to wildlife. Squirrels, mice, voles, and deer relish them. Country gardeners can pretty much skip planting them unless they have deer fencing. In my experience, tulips don't need to be planted as deep as is usually recommended. Four or five inches deep is just fine for the hybrids, with about two or three for the species. This rule of thumb works out consistently for almost all bulbs. Crocus, snowdrops, snow iris, and grape hyacinth are a breeze to plant. I prefer to scatter a dozen or so at a time (for an unstudied, natural look) and then pop them into the soil with a dandelion digger or Japanese fisherman's knife.

If rodents are a problem in your area, grow those tasty tulip bulbs in pots that you can more easily protect during the winter.

Since I'm so picky about tulips, you might expect the same treatment for the other bulbs. Here goes, but it's much simpler. Most daffodils work well in garden soil that stays moderately moist. Thankfully, daffodils are poisonous and repel most pests. Deer may nibble them but generally leave them alone. The classic yellow daffodils we all love such as 'Unsurpassable', 'Golden Harvest', and 'Dutch Master' are tops on my list as well as white 'Ice Follies' and very fragrant white 'Thalia'. I'm also crazy about the old-fashioned 'Pheasant's Eye', with white petals and a small, red-edged cup and a green eye, and I love the classic miniature or Cyclamineus daffodils such as yellow 'Tete-a-Tete' and 'February Gold', yellow with orange trumpet 'Jetfire', as well as white 'Toto'. The latter is touted as the white 'Tete-a-Tete'—but hey, wasn't Toto a little black terrier?

Hyacinths will probably stick around for many years in your garden, although the flower heads will be a bit smaller and less top-heavy than in their first season. I adore the fragrance of hyacinths, and I have never met an ugly one. All the pink, blue, and purple ones are wonderful, but for something slightly different, try yellow 'City of Haarlem' or apricot 'Gypsy Queen'. 'Hollyhock' is a lovely, special hyacinth heirloom with double, raspberry-red flowers. The multiflora types seem more graceful and loose than the standard types as they produce multiple stems of white, pink, or pale blue flowers. 'Festival Pink' is especially fragrant.

The smaller, so-called minor bulbs may be short in stature, but they're long on charm. I can't think of any problems that you might encounter with them. Snowdrops usually bloom first in my garden (vying with the crocus) with their pendant, pristine white flowers popping up in the shady areas where they thrive best. Snow crocus such as pale 'Blue Pearl' or yellow 'Goldilocks' may be a bit smaller than the jumbo Dutch crocus but they multiply quickly. They are beautiful naturalized in either a buffalo grass or traditional lawn. Sweet-scented snow iris—just inches tall with purple, blue, or white blossoms—possess all the beauty of their giant, bearded cousins that flower in May. Siberian squills mimic the sky and have seeded throughout my garden, contrasting with the pale striped squill (*Pushkinia*) and blue, pink, or white glory-of-the-snow (*Chionodoxa*) that likewise have made themselves at home.

Overly tidy gardeners don't appreciate these friendly self-sowing bulbs, but I cherish them for popping up unexpectedly and covering big bare patches such as beneath shrubs and trees. If you own a crabapple, please plant grape hyacinths beneath it. The blossoms of the two usually coincide and pink crabapple petals falling on the blue hyacinths is one of my favorite sights of spring. Add some vinca to create a carpet and some daffodils and you've got the recipe for enchantment.

What you combine with bulbs makes the difference between "nice" and "wow." That's where ground-cover perennials come into play. Bulbs emerge easily through their mats of foliage and look much more beautiful with companions than against bare earth. Creeping phlox, Turkish and creeping veronica, shorter sedums, thymes, vinca, basket-of-gold, sweet woodruff, and many others make great bulb companions. These early flowers rank among the most lovely of the garden, justifying our fall planting efforts.

"Re-merchandizing"

A friend who used to manage a clothing store dropped by as I was reworking and rearranging my containers in early fall.

"You're re-merchandizing, I see," he said. I had no idea what he was talking about, never having worked in retail, but he explained how stores re-arrange displays. In fall, for example, after the hottest new clothes have been picked over, the store rearranges the displays to put on a fresh face.

Once I learned about re-merchandizing, I realized that I do it several times a year, but especially in fall. The "picked-over" plants get moved or composted, while pots that are looking especially good get the spotlight. Inexpensive mums and asters appear at garden centers and discount stores. I really enjoy reworking container groupings to feature them. I especially like buying a half-dozen mums in the same color to enhance one area, and a half-dozen more in a different shade for another spot.

My favorite part of fall re-merchandizing is adding pumpkins and squash. My linden tree adds yellow leaves. I fill my antique wheelbarrow with the pretty crop of pumpkins. The old turquoise paint of the wheelbarrow is a great contrast. Pumpkins, gourds, and mums look wonderful in every setting, but I prefer not to go too Halloween crazy. I carve a few for the big day, but I like their presence for the entire season. I traded a bumper crop of tomatoes for a neighbor's equally bountiful crop of gourds. I'm crazy about gourds. However, I don't really have space for them, so trading is perfect. I grouped them in baskets and piles all over the patio. I encrusted the patio table with them, surrounding a centerpiece of kale. When I had friends

over for chili on a chilly evening, I forced them to eat outside, moving just enough of the gourds to fit in the dishes. They got out cameras to capture the moment; it's not often that one is forced to dine in the table arrangement.

I've actually gotten rather notorious for my organic table displays, usually involving fruit, vegetables, flowers, leaves, branches, and moss. They are, at least, a distraction from any shortcomings of my cuisine.

Late Fall
- pot up forced bulbs
- blow out sprinklers
- coil and store hoses
- turn off water lines as necessary to prevent spigots from freezing
- gather and store tools
- protect vulnerable plants

Forcing Bulbs

Sometimes gardeners buy too many bulbs and can't get them in the ground before winter settles in. There's a solution other than chipping through frozen soil with an ice pick. Pot them up to have beautiful flowers on your winter windowsill. They'll arrive before spring does. The practice of potting and chilling bulbs to bloom ahead of schedule is called "forcing." It's really more like gentle persuasion. If you pot up spring-flowering tulips, daffodils, and hyacinths in late fall, you can get them to flower early on the winter windowsill or spring patio. Gardeners become ravenous for color in late winter and early spring. The heady scent of hyacinths or pots of cheerful

Pumpkins, gourds, and falling leaves make me appreciate the last few months of the growing season rather than allowing myself to fall into a melancholy mode.

crocus work wonders as antidotes to the blues.

Forcing bulbs is easy. Nearly every kind of spring-flowering bulbs can be coaxed into bloom in pots weeks or even months ahead of their garden-planted counterparts. Nurseries customarily mark down their bulb stocks in late November and early December, enticing farsighted gardeners to go overboard. Count me in; last year I forced about a hundred pots of bulbs. You may wish to start with a manageable dozen or so.

Look for bargain bags of fifty or more tulip or daffodil bulbs. They'll fill several very large pots or a half dozen smaller ones to make a spectacular show. You can also experiment with crocus, squills, grape hyacinths, and glory-of-the-snow. Most any type of container will do as long as it has a drainage hole. Terra-cotta pots are traditional, but you may also use glazed or fiberglass pots. Plastic pots work quite well and, if you object to their looks, you can hide them in a decorative basket or cachepot at blooming time. Use the deepest pots for daffodils as they put out the most extensive root systems.

Once you've hit the nursery sales, assemble bulbs, pots, and soil where you've got plenty of elbow room. I just spread a sheet on the kitchen floor and get to work. Fill each pot about two-thirds full with potting soil. Set the bulbs on the soil with their sides just touching and cover with a few inches of soil, patting it down firmly with your palms. Insert a plastic label or mark the side of the pot with the variety and planting date. Don't water at this point since you've first got to find a "forcing chamber" for the newly potted bulbs.

This is the tricky part. The place you house these has got to be dark and relatively cold—at least 40 degrees. The reason why you don't see tulips and daffodils in California or Florida is that it's simply too warm. Spring-flowering bulbs require a winter chilling to induce flowering. They start to root the minute you plant them, pumping moisture to the bulb after a long dry spell out of the ground. The smaller bulbs will be ready to flower in as little as ten weeks, while the larger bulbs generally require twelve to sixteen weeks, depending on your individual conditions. Utilize your crawlspace, unheated garage, or shed to house your bulbs. I once used a very cold closet in a former house. No suitable spot? Dig a trench in the garden, set the pots inside, and mulch with plenty of leaves or straw.

After your potted bulbs are in place, water generously. I keep mine in plastic trays to make this easier. Check on them once a month and add water as needed. The idea is to keep them moist but not soggy. Temperatures just a few degrees above freezing are ideal for forcing, but that's difficult to maintain. Even if temperatures slip into the single digits for a short time, your bulbs will probably be fine. If the winter is especially cold and you're using an unheated garage or shed, you may wish to add the extra protection of old blankets on top the pots. Mice like crocus and tulips, but leave most other bulbs alone. One of my cats, Kitty Carlisle, is an excellent mouser, so I put her on duty in the garage where I force most of my bulbs.

Keep an eye on the calendar. After ten or twelve weeks, white roots should be showing through the drainage holes of the pots and shoots should be emerging. When plants reach an inch in height above soil, you can bring them indoors to a very bright window. Keep them moist, and they'll bloom within a week or two. I hold most of mine as long as possible and then bring them out to the patio. They can handle nightly frosts easily, but I take the pots back into the garage if it snows to prevent the flower stems from snapping.

Your outdoor display can be even lovelier if you enhance it with pots of other frost-tolerant early flowers such as pansies, dianthus, snapdragons, and Persian buttercups. Use upturned pots or cement blocks to vary the heights of the containers. Wheelbarrows and wagons really show them off as a grouping. Keep the bulbs moist as the buds bloom. Fertilize if you intend to recycle the bulbs by planting them in the garden. You can plant them "in the green" directly out of the pot after they finish flowering or wait until the foliage has completely withered and browned. With just a bit of extra care, they can be restored to their full glory to provide many beautiful springs.

Thanksgiving Décor

Seasonal plants, fruit, and flowers can enhance your Thanksgiving dinner, making it a memorable event. Consider cut flowers, potted plants, and fruit for table centerpieces or to decorate your mantle, breakfront, or buffet table.

Mums and other potted flowers such as hydrangeas and ornamental peppers are popular this time of year. To make

I go all-out with natural holiday decorations, once forcing guests to eat a chili supper on my gourd-encrusted patio table topped by sunflowers and kale.

their presentation special, insert their pots into a creative container such as a soup tureen or pumpkin. A pumpkin can also serve as a unique vase (it will hold water) for a bouquet of mums, daisies, and carnations. You may want to pick the seed heads of ornamental grasses or rose hips from your garden to add to cut-flower arrangements. Miniature pumpkins or gourds can easily be put to use for small flowers. Cut out a small hole at the top and scoop out the contents with a small spoon. These little bouquets may be set on each guest's plate. Mini pumpkins can also be employed as candleholders.

You can create a dramatic pumpkin topiary, stacking three pumpkins of diminishing size on top of one another. Insert a sturdy wooden dowel (from the hardware store) into a pot of sand or soil. Cut holes in the top and bottom of the two largest pumpkins and place over the dowel. The top pumpkin needs only a bottom hole and then complete the stack.

You can also accent your table with gourds, squash, and fresh fruit such as pomegranates, apples, oranges, and pears, as well as nuts. They look lovely nestled in a basket, traditional cornucopia, or favorite bowl. Try filling a large glass jar or vase with pretty fruit to truly showcase their forms and colors. Cranberries look beautiful in a clear vase holding stems of seasonal flowers. The berries will stay fresh in the water for several weeks. All of this can be done ahead of time to allow you to cook and enjoy the day.

Ivy or rosemary topiaries in the shapes of balls or cones can also be placed on tables and mantles. These living geo-metric forms add a formal touch to your celebration. Keep them slightly moist (never soggy), provide bright light, and these plants can continue to enhance your home for upcoming holidays.

Hanukkah Flowers

Many families observe Hanukkah by lighting candles on the menorah, a nine-branched candelabra, as the center of the celebration. You can enhance your Hanukkah by using traditional colors, cut flowers, and other natural winter materials.

Silver, white, and dark blue are colors that have come to be associated with Hanukkah. You can make your home special by showcasing vases, bowls, and goblets of cobalt blue, crystal, and silver. The emphasis is on shiny surfaces that reflect candlelight. A grouping of several vases or bowls of different sizes and shapes can be displayed on a silver or mirrored tray, or perhaps on a shiny glass or marble table surface.

Simple arrangements of seasonal flowers can be beautiful and elegant in these containers. Look for white forms of favorite winter cut flowers such as mums, daisies, lilies, baby's breath, snapdragons, and alstroemeria, as well as potted paperwhites or white amaryllis. You can supplement these with branches and greenery from your garden such as willow, maples, and juniper.

Consider floating cut flowers such as lilies or mums in a pretty bowl. This not only stretches the effectiveness of your cut flowers, but the flowers last longer. This presentation is restrained and elegant.

Centerpieces

Millions of poinsettias grace homes each holiday season. Come January, millions of them will end up in dumpsters and compost heaps. Not many people have the patience to keep these cheerful red heralds of the season growing after New Year's Day, but with a little care they will perform better and last longer. In addition, they can be combined with other seasonal plants to create more beautiful, memorable holiday displays.

Few things are as sad as a neglected poinsettia encased in shiny foil that has lost all its leaves, with just a few sticks supporting the last of its flowers. When you purchase these traditional plants this season, liberate them from the foil wrapping when you get home. The foil prevents the pot from draining, setting up a lethal case of overwatering. As leaves drop (which they will, in response to the lower humidity and light in your house), our natural inclination is to pour on the water until we drown the poor thing. To prevent this, set the pot in a saucer and water only when the soil is dry to the touch. Keep the plant away from heat ducts to help prevent desiccation.

Hybridizers have created interesting new introductions over the past decade, so that the standard red poinsettia has been transformed. Salmon pink, ivory, and plum forms have become nearly as common as the traditional red, as well as ones with polka dots and streaks. These invite creative new combinations with other seasonal plants. My favorite way to display them is in a very large basket with plants with other colors and textures.

Stick to the traditional red, white, and green scheme or branch out to suit your taste and décor.

Poinsettias dominate any display, but they can be interestingly contrasted by foliage plants such as English ivy, ferns, Norfolk Island pine, dracaenas, and pothos. The real fun, however, comes from combining poinsettias with the other seasonal flowers that they tend to overshadow. Amaryllis and paperwhite narcissus have great presence and a long history associated with the holidays. Other lovely flowering plants include mums, azaleas, hydrangea, gloxinia, and kalanchoe. If you're truly adventurous, consider camellia, gardenia, or dwarf citrus trees, although you'll need good light and high humidity to help them adapt to your home in the long run.

Other winter-bloomers deserve consideration for holiday display. Tops on my list is the Christmas cactus. This is an easy, long-term houseplant that may live for decades with good care, which basically means ignoring it. The Christmas cactus plants available today are hybrids from two different, related kinds of cactus found growing in the mountains near Rio de Janeiro in Brazil. The bright color of the flaring, tubular flowers suggests a carnival in Rio, dazzling us with near-neon shades of red, magenta, orange, pink, and white.

Unlike most plants that have discernable stems and leaves, a Christmas cactus is composed solely of flattened, succulent stems that look like the plant world's version of Legos. As they grow and arch, they take on an architectural grace, so that the plant remains handsome

My holiday decorations are strictly for the birds, and perhaps a few squirrels, who feast on strings of popcorn and cranberries, shredded wheat ornaments and peanut butter and birdseed-coated pinecones.

even when not in bloom. Many people choose to grow them in hanging baskets.

A Christmas cactus makes an ideal subject for negligent gardeners. All it needs is a bright spot, plus water and water-soluble fertilizer only several times a month. When the plant sets bud in fall, keep it evenly moist throughout its blooming period. Then stop watering for a month and then go back to watering and fertilizing every few weeks. Your plant will likely rebud and bloom again at Easter and perhaps again in early summer. You can give your plant a summer vacation outdoors—but not in

I don't cut back perennials until late winter. In the meantime, I console myself indoors with winter-blooming houseplants.

hot, burning sun since its native habitat is somewhat shady and moist. The plants can stand to get quite pot bound, but eventually will need to be moved up to a larger size. In time a plant may reach the size of a bushel basket and bear hundreds of flowers at a time.

Cyclamen are sometimes called Persian violets and grow wild in the eastern Mediterranean region, including Greece and Turkey. The plants grow from potato-like tubers and usually go dormant during the heat of summer. They revel in cool weather, sending up pretty rounded leaves marbled with silver markings. The upside-down flowers are quite unusual in the plant world, with the opening at the bottom and the petals flung upward. They look somewhat like hovering butterflies and are borne in winter. This makes them a great choice for both the holidays and the dull days of January and February.

Cyclamen flowers rival those of Christmas cactus for brilliance. They are available in red, salmon, magenta, violet, pale pink, and white, often with a contrasting ring. Miniature varieties are also available. The flowers of some plants bear a lovely fragrance, while others offer nothing at all. Let your nose be your guide when you buy cyclamens. The keys to growing them well are to never let them dry out while they're in bloom and to keep them in a bright, cool location at around 50 to 60 degrees. My drafty Victorian house is ideal. If your home is more energy-efficient, keep them in the coolest spot you can find away from heat registers.

Although many people simply toss their cyclamens after blooming, you can keep them going, knowing they won't look their best in summer. In May, bring the pots outdoors and put them in bright shade. Water only sparingly. The plants may go dormant during the heat of summer, but keep them slightly moist. When fall arrives, step up the moisture and begin to feed. By next December, the beautiful flowers may return.

Baskets of pretty seasonal plants make great gifts. It's easy to create a traditional one with red and white flowers and interesting greenery. A pastel-themed basket might include salmon pink poinsettias, white or pink azaleas, pink cyclamen, orange-red Christmas cactus, the huge trumpets of white and pink 'Appleblossom' amaryllis, white variegated ivy, and fine-textured pine. Fill the gaps between pots with crumpled newspaper and disguise with moss. For a finishing touch, tuck in pinecones. When I was a kid, we used to paint the tips of the cones with white shoe polish to simulate snow. It seems that might be just the thing for this combination, mixing old traditions with new sensibilities.

When January arrives, assess your plants to see how they've fared. If they've received adequate light and been watered faithfully, most should look fairly decent. With the exception of the paperwhites, which are usually discarded, all of them can be grown on indefinitely. Perhaps you won't be able to bear the sight of a poinsettia after New Year's Day. Feel free to chuck it. But some people like the challenge of keeping it alive. Remember that this Mexican native likes bright light and can't stand drought. Cut off the remaining flowers and prune the branches back by several inches. Fertilize to encourage new growth. It should respond with bushy new foliage. Consider giving it a vacation outside next summer.

Will it bloom again? That's up to you. Greenhouse growers go through a complicated process to induce their poinsettias to bloom for sale. The plants respond to a reduction in light in fall to produce the colorful bracts that resemble petals, with the actual flowers being very small. The time-honored directions for re-blooming involve setting the plant in a dark closet, starting in September, at four in the afternoon and taking it out again at sunrise. It can't have one ray of light during this time, not even from a streetlight. I know of only one home gardener who has actually re-bloomed a poinsettia, and that was quite by accident. She kept her plant in a hot-tub room at the back of the house. After the sun set each day, it was in complete darkness. The red flowers came as a delightful December surprise. Perhaps it will happen for you.

Gifts for Gardeners

Like most people, gardeners appreciate gifts that are either beautiful or usable. Beauty's subjective. It would be difficult for all gardeners to arrive at a consensus as to what makes a garden-worthy ornament. As the recipient of numerous garden ornaments, my sincere advice is to avoid giving them. What you, as the gift-giver, might find too precious for words may make the receiver cringe to display it in his or her garden.

Stick to the truly beautiful—plants. I can't imagine a gardener of any skill level who wouldn't be delighted with a blooming gift. Orchids, African violets, cyclamen, and other winter-blooming plants are always welcome to a house-bound gardener. I'm especially fond of miniature citrus trees because of their deliciously scented flowers and ease of culture. I'm wild about Christmas cactus as well, since they are exceedingly difficult to kill and flower faithfully every winter. Herbal topiaries add an architectural note of interest to any décor, from country French to minimalist modernism. The sculptural qualities of bonsai plants have a timeless appeal. Gardeners with a passion for a particular kind of plant will be pleased with a purchase or gift certificate from a specialist grower.

Useful gifts for the gardener include tools, articles of clothing, pots, and remedies for their perpetual cuts, stings, and aching muscles. Remember that gardeners value quality and you can't go wrong with practical items that they use on a nearly daily basis during the growing season. Because I tend to lose small implements, you'd never find me "re-gifting" items such as a trowel, dandelion digger, Japanese fisherman's knife, soil scoop, or watering wand. The only small tool I've yet to lose is a three-pronged claw that is in mint condition because I never use it. Skip buying one of those. Even though I have a tool shed, my tools never seem to be in it. A freestanding or wall organizer for tools would be ideal for the busy gardener.

Three higher-end tools that any gardener would welcome are a border spade, digging fork, and a quality pair of pruners. Quality versions don't come cheap, but may last a lifetime. A sturdy standard hoe or horseshoe-shaped shuffle hoe may prove invaluable as well. Check the construction of tools before you buy. I once had a hoe that often separated at the point where the shank met the handle. I glued, screwed, and clamped the worthless tool way too many times before I finally threw it away. If only I'd started with a well-built hoe I could have avoided a lot of bother.

Gardeners can be hard on their gloves. Rose growers would love a puncture-proof pair of leather gloves in March and April when pruning gets into full swing. Insulated gloves prove valuable in colder months. Washable, lighter-weight gloves with rubberized fingers and palms also come in handy at planting time. New "bionic" gloves aid gardeners with arthritis. I regularly lose and abuse gloves. I'm also tough on wide-rimmed sun hats that I ruin on an annual basis.

Give pots. No gardener can have too many. A pretty glazed ceramic pot—perhaps in cobalt blue, oxblood red, or celadon green—will serve for decades and become a constant reminder of Christmas past. Several of my pots remind me of the special people who gave them to me and they hold my very best plants. Vases may be a bit more difficult to select. Depending on the gardener's personal style, I'd suggest a pretty crystal rose bowl to float flowers or a pretty pitcher to hold a country-style arrangement.

Though gardeners may enjoy their winter retirement, in a few months they'll be back to digging, planting, and pruning. With that come aches, scrapes, and stings. We can all appreciate a soothing herbal bath and lotions and balms for calluses, insect bites, and beat-up cuticles. Gardeners also enjoy bird-watching during their winter vacations. Attracting birds to the garden helps with insect control. A book on bird identification is helpful for gardeners of all ages as they watch these creatures flock to feeders. A bird feeder makes a great focal point situated near a kitchen or office window, wherever a gardener spends a lot of time. Stuff a stocking with bird seed. Gardeners appreciate the nongerminating mixes that don't sprout into a crop of millet and sorghum below the feeder come spring. A durable metal bucket with lid stores bird seed in the garage or porch, safe from mice. To really pamper our feathered friends, a birdbath heater provides drinking water and a bracing bath when other sources have frozen over.

Dish Gardens

With kids home for the holidays, mom and dad often need to find fun projects for them to do. When I was a boy, I found it fascinating to create a miniature world in a dish garden. I still do. Kids enjoy making and caring for these small gardens that they can keep in their bedroom windows.

Start with a wide, shallow pot with a drainage hole and a saucer to fit it. Some kids may like planting a little jungle or forest, while others might enjoy a desert landscape. You'll find small, inexpensive

houseplants at your local garden center. Consider ivies, palms, false aralia, creeping fig, and ferns, as well as small African violets, cactus, and succulents.

Fill the pot nearly all the way with potting soil and begin to plant. You can space the plants close together. Work in rocks and driftwood to simulate boulders and fallen trees. Finish off this miniscape with pebbles or gravel, or add marbles or seashells. You can also decorate your miniature landscape with small statuary or figurines. Perhaps dinosaurs rampage through the vegetation, or maybe wolves, deer, cats, or unicorns. Frogs or toads can sun themselves on the rocks. Or maybe ballerinas dance through the miniature forest. Let your child's imagination populate this little landscape.

A dish garden composed of common houseplants can survive in any bright room and doesn't necessarily need to be placed in direct sun. A garden with cactus and succulents will probably do best in a sunny west- or south-facing window, where beautiful flowers may surprise your child. With either type of dish garden, water only when the soil becomes dry. Fertilize only sparingly or the plants will soon outgrow their miniature charm.

You don't need to be a kid to enjoy dish gardens. Designing and planting these can be a fun winter activity for grown-up gardeners, too. Once planted, they can be especially pleasing in bathrooms, on kitchen windowsills, and in breakfast nooks.

Chapter Three

Artistry with the Ordinary

*N*ew plant introductions in the green industry cost big bucks. It's all about supply and demand. The newest coral bell or lily hybrids, limited in quantity until stocks build up, command premium prices. I drool over them in catalogs and at the garden center and wait for the day when they go from extravagant to affordable. Usually, it takes a couple of years. When those gorgeous coral bells with maroon leaves splashed with silver debuted in the '90s, such as 'Pewter Veil' and 'Plum Pudding', they were quite pricey. This spring they showed up in the garden section of a local discount home improvement store.

Ordinary plants weave together artistically, with dwarf baby's breath frothing softly amongst pink Mexican evening primrose, catmint and fleabane daisy.

A view to the garden from the patio is framed by potted peach geraniums, lavender cape daisies, and the first flowers of canna 'Louis Cotton.'

The apricot flowers of 'Louis Cotton' top bronze-green foliage and effectively contrast those of a variegated flowering maple.

Similarly, bulb prices dip when supplies rise. Lily varieties such as crimson-maroon 'Black Beauty' and rosy 'Stargazer' were once out of reach for many budgets, but slowly became more common and affordable as more growing fields were devoted to them. The terrific allium 'Globemaster', a lovely ornamental onion hailed for its large round globes of lavender-purple flowers, once cost more than twenty dollars for a single bulb. Its advantage is that its flowers are sterile and therefore longer-lasting since they don't fade after getting pollinated as most flowers do. 'Globemaster' bulbs, though still not as inexpensive as tulips, are much more affordable today. The canna 'Stuttgart', a designer's dream with its white-striped foliage, was once seen only in the gardens of the elite. I found it this spring at a garden center with a reasonable eight-dollar price tag. Another canna I've long admired, 'Louis Cotton,' was once an elusive prize. I balked at the price tag in catalogs even though I'm nuts about the bronze-green leaves topped by apricot flowers. I spied gallon potted plants by chance at a home improvement center for just over three dollars a pot.

The trellis was brand new when I took this shot in June and the morning glory seedlings hadn't yet started their climb. I've since planted both roses and clematis to cloak it.

There's always something new. Perennials are reborn in new colors or with variegated or golden leaves. Hybridists must work with the diligence of NASA engineers to develop the daylilies, dahlias, hostas, and roses that tempt us each spring. I'm not immune to temptation. Sometimes I decide that new tires can be put off a little bit longer (that excuse is starting to endanger motorists throughout the greater metro area) so that I can spring for a new introduction. The splurges add a little spice to my garden's mix.

Golden Oldies

Every plant in my garden was at one time a new horticultural introduction. I wasn't alive when many of them first came into cultivation. The golden age was the Victorian era, when wealthy men and botanic gardens such as Kew in London sent explorers around the globe to seek out new species. From China, Africa, India, and Australia came incredible wonders of nature that still bear some of the names of these explorers (or the patrons that bankrolled them) such as *Hosta sieboldiana*, named for the German plant enthusiast Philipp Franz von Siebold, or *Lilium henryi*, honoring Dr. A. Henry, a plant collector who gathered species in China at the end of the nineteenth century.

Many of these plants are now considered old stalwarts, the basics that we build our gardens around. Familiarity breeds contempt. Even really great plants, such as 'Autumn Joy' sedum, go from being prominent to passé as the years go by, eventually showing up in parking lot

People whose yarrow gets out of control water it too much. People who let Queen Anne's lace bloom in their garden are crazy unless they judiciously deadhead.

plantings in stripmalls. I occasionally hear people in nurseries dismiss a plant, uttering, "That old thing," as if they'd stepped in dog doo. I'd hate for them to come to my garden. It's full of old things (and dogs). I love them all. The trick is to make art out of the ordinary.

Putting it Together

To me, gardening is an art. A dirty, sweaty one—but an art all the same. Painters don't get new color introductions to work with every spring. They create something new and original from an existing palette. A gardener can do the same. (Of course,

painters don't have to worry about one of their colors dying over the winter.) Many great plants have stood the test of time. They belong in our gardens whether our budgets are big or small. Because they're frequently considered mundane, these classic plants (and I'm talking primarily about perennials; we'll get to annuals later) don't carry high price tags or get top billing at the nursery. Often these plants are available in smaller, budget-size quarts and "tuna quarters." Friends, neighbors, and relatives will often be glad to give you a hunk of a nice, vigorous yarrow, daylily, or lamium, examples of such garden standbys.

Gardening with the ordinary begins with observing what wants to grow in your area. Don't look at the best gardens first; instead, look at the worst. In unkempt, untended yards you'll see what thrives, despite neglect. Discover what's surviving the rigors of life in the alley, too. You might want to see what's blooming in the Burger King parking lot, as long as you don't emulate the design. Even highway median strips offer possibilities.

When you're on a shoestring budget, you're not likely to assemble all your plants at one time. The process is very different in my own garden, for example, than it is in a client's garden, where a truck delivers what I order and I put the plants into place. By the way, I draw only the crudest of plans, not official-looking blueprints that look great on the coffee table but rarely translate into a beautiful

garden. I order an assortment of plants that I know well and that are suitable for the site. From experience, I know they can be combined artfully to create a pretty picture. Then I let them "tell" me where they should go. This process is very loosely orchestrated, but relatively quick if my muses are really jamming. At home in my own garden, the plants arrive in fits and starts, depending on my modest budget, bargains, and donations from fellow gardeners. My muses and I can only guess what the next arrival might be. So I work with what's here, making designs from remnants. It's a patchwork. And I rather enjoy the challenge.

When new plants come into my possession, I carry them around the garden to see with what other plants they'd go best. I don't look for bare holes. That's a bad habit to get into, for soon your garden will look like the dog's dinner. Consider height, spread, foliage color, and growth characteristics—and, of course, bloom color and shape. There will probably be more possibilities than you imagine, since a new plant can often go either in front of or behind an existing one with very different effect. If the plant has a fine texture, it will likely show best when contrasted against a plant with bigger, bolder leaves. I brought home a new yarrow several days ago, one I thought sounded good (it's only several inches tall so I'm trusting the tag that 'Royal Robe' is a pretty, deep lavender-purple). I wandered around for a while,

I'm not certain of the identity of these roses since they came with the place and I transplanted them. Companions include larkspur, Jupiter's beard, salvia, and snow daisies.

The grapefruit-size heads of star-of-Persia
(Allium christophii) *add a whimsical touch*
in early summer and even the dried seed heads
add great texture later.

looking for possible companions. Yarrows are easy to situate since they have finely cut leaves, dependable flowers, and iron constitutions. My first inclination was to pair it with something yellow, but not too bright. I planted it next to the pale yellow pincushion flower (*Scabiosa ochroleuca*) and stood back to envision how they'd look together. Good, I thought.

Then I began to notice that the color of 'Royal Robe' would probably get lost in the blue haze of a drift of 'Walker's Low' catmint behind the two. "That won't do," I muttered and resolved to do some reorganizing. About ten feet away is the

lovely shrub rose 'Morden Sunrise'. Its pointed orange buds open to stunning pale tangerine and yellow single flowers. I didn't actually say "Aha!" (although I do sometimes talk to myself aloud in the garden), but I knew where the yarrow should go—and the yellow scabiosa. After some transplanting, the rose got some new companions. It just occurred to me that a drift of 'Pikes Peak Purple' penstemons (say that aloud three times really fast) might be just the thing to plant in front of the yellow pincushion flowers. Then I'm going to fish around for something orange, low, and rounded to skirt the penstemons—or perhaps some chartreuse lady's mantle. I've got a bit of moving and digging yet to do before this vignette satisfies me.

Gardens are meant to change, from week to week as well as from year to year. It's like a patchwork quilt you never finish. With a little experience, you'll develop an instinct for good combinations. Be willing to move plants around. In most regions it's not wise to do this in the heat of summer, so you might consider a holding bed for plants that come to you in July and August. This will give you more time to consider future companions. I sometimes pass an area in my garden and wonder what I was thinking when I put a particular combination together. Maybe the colors don't work as I'd intended, or the textures are too similar. I'll make a note to change it when I can; perhaps something else should be added to it to make the combination pop. I heard a story many years ago that really changed the way I put

Red and orange touches blaze throughout the garden, with big red umbrellas
perhaps giving the impression that I'm operating a Mexican restaurant.

plants together. It concerned a woman who had slaved over her garden, creating artful color schemes. Still she wasn't satisfied. She hired a noted garden designer

Rob's 35 Amazing Ordinary Plants

Baby's breath
Bachelor's button
Ballota
Bread seed poppy
Bumblebee daisy
California poppy
Catmint
Clary sage
Clematis integrifolia
Cottage pinks
Creeping phlox
Cupid's dart
Daylily
Dragon's blood sedum
Dusty meadow rue
Giant sea kale
Gloriosa daisy
Iris
Lamb's ears
Larkspur
Meadow sage
Nasturtium
Ponytail grass
Purple coneflower
Rue
Sedum 'Autumn Joy'
Shrub roses
Snow daisy
Sunflower
Sunrose
Tall verbena
Thyme
Valerian
Yarrow
Yellow columbine

to critique it. He surveyed her borders carefully and finally said simply, "Madam, all of your leaves are the same size."

I've given leaves a great deal of thought since then. I consider not only their size but also their colors and patina, meaning whether they're smooth, shiny, hairy, or crinkled. Many fine flowering plants have unremarkable leaves. I use these for their flower colors and shapes, then blend in plants with extraordinary foliage to make the flowers look even better. Here's an example from my garden. A grouping with the satin ribbon pink mallow (*Malva alcea*), the yellow columbine 'Denver Gold', and some purple iris was nice but not terribly exciting. I added seedlings of the annual red orach (*Atriplex hortensis* 'Rubra'), which has foliage the color of cooked beets, and the area started to intrigue me. Then my friend Lena, who works at a nursery, insisted I try her favorite rose, the rugosa 'Dash's Dart', with violet pink, deliciously fragrant flowers. The rose petals echo the maroon orach and harmonize with the pink mallow. A week later I bought three seedlings of the golden-leafed hyssop (*Hyssopus officinalis* 'Golden Jubilee'), which has lavender-pink spikes of flowers. With some rearranging, the vibrant rose and the chartreuse foliage of the hyssop made the pink/yellow/maroon combination more complex and interesting. The chartreuse gives highlights to the grouping, whereas the maroon orach foliage adds depth and shadow. The brighter, deeper rose has become the star, with the mallow and columbine

Busy bees have crossed my stand of yellow columbines with other species in the neighborhood, resulting in multi-colored offspring. I bought the little blue spruce; the rest of the plants are from seed or division.

much better in supporting roles. Topping it off, I transplanted some blue catmint seedlings to the front of this ensemble. Now it pops.

The Core

Self-sown seedlings are the greatest boon for the budget-conscious gardener since compost. My garden is based around about twenty species of perennials that I dug from my previous garden (which I left intact), one clump of iris that was growing near the front porch of my house (before it fell down), an unidentified shrub rose crammed in near the old driveway (before I demolished it), and a dozen or so carefree, self-sowing annuals. I created an entire garden from these 35 species of plants for the cost of the seed packets, not to mention the time required to dig and transplant them. I've added to the mix as my checkbook allows, focusing mainly on perennials and some shrubs.

*Snow daisy (*Tanacetum niveum*) finds my garden exactly to its liking. A short-lived perennial, it seeds itself abundantly; nobody leaves my garden without seedlings.*

Around that core of plants, I've added many perennials that I've either grown from seed or purchased as very small plants. I'm lucky to live near a small mom-and-pop nursery that's been growing plants since the '40s. They don't have the latest, priciest perennials, but they do offer homegrown, old-fashioned perennials that they propagate either from seed or division. I imagine walking into this little nursery in 1950 and finding pretty near the same selection of plants that are there today. Most are in quarts or tuna quarters, while the best (and cheapest) are in shallow pans with about a dozen seedlings. These little seedlings need to be gently teased apart and carefully tended during their infancy, but they develop amazingly fast. They'll thrive best if planted in the cool, damp weather of midspring.

Imagine getting a half-dozen red Oriental poppies for $2.19. I planted those last spring and they'll reward me already this year with a smattering of fiery blossoms. I've also bought other tiny perennials from this nursery that have panned out well: blue flax, several species of penstemon, fleabane daisy (*Erigeron speciosus*), coral bells, pinks, yarrow, and saponaria. It takes nimble fingers and patience to work with these delicate young plants. Dig an ample little hole, perhaps 5 inches deep and 3 inches wide. Hold the seedling gently, dangling the roots into the hole while you slowly refill it. Form a small earthen dike around the plant and then "puddle" it in so that the root-ball is thoroughly saturated. Keep it continuously moist for the next month as the roots take hold, gradually easing off the water.

At the rate of $1.49 for a 4-inch pot, I've also covered a lot of ground with perennials divided from their perennial stock, such as ice plants, thyme, lamium, 'Clara Curtis' daisy, asters, and sedum acre. I can only hope that Al's Pine Garden stays in business for a very long time (though Al himself is long gone and they don't sell pines anymore). I also hope you'll find a similar gem in your neighborhood or town.

With Friends Like That, Who Needs Anemones?

In my previous gardens, I've always had a fine stand of Japanese anemone. Though there are a number of cultivars available, ranging from white to deep pink flowers, often doubled, I like the old-fashioned single pink form (*Anemone vitifolia* 'Robustissima'). Sadly, the sole wholesale grower in my region seems to have dropped this variety from its list. I'll track some down eventually. I'm already envisioning where a swath should go, with its pink flowers backed by a young blue spruce. The anemones will arrive in good time. In the meantime, I'm not about to leave a bare spot, so I'm visiting my friends' gardens and hoping for handouts.

Not everybody is lucky enough to have a previous garden from which to take seedlings and cuttings. That's what friends are for. There's nothing wrong with some

It took three years and about $300 to create my nearly over-stuffed garden, with many old-fashioned perennials starting as very small plants from local nurseries.

talk around your coworkers and relatives about how hard you're working in your garden. Display your dirty nails, cuts, and calluses on cue, then wring your hands when you discuss the high prices at your local nursery. Then compliment them on that lovely yellow iris you've always admired in their backyard.

Gardeners, as a general rule, are a generous lot. It's in their nature to nurture, whether it's seedlings or struggling fellow gardeners. We're passionate about plants and keen to share them with people who'll like them as much as we do. Last spring I attended a wedding shower for my friend Angie, who was starting both a marriage and a garden. My present was a pickup truck load of freshly dug seedling snow daisies, meadow sage, valerian, and catmint, as well as sacks of iris tubers. Even my young garden had produced plenty to share. Neighbors and visitors who express an interest in something go home with seedlings or at least a promise for a "start" of something when the timing is right.

Flower gifts from friends and relatives become more special as time passes. The association with a favorite person sometimes even elevates a plant in our estimation

The brilliant pink heads of Dianthus giganteus *float above a pastel pastiche of lamb's ear and catmint.*

Before I planted dwarf Alberta spruce in the pots lining my path I used annuals but they got lost in the shuffle.

My friend Angie gave me a packet of red sunflower seeds that I planted in the narrow strip between the fence and sidewalk, creating a towering hedge.

to heights beyond what it truly deserves. We overlook a proclivity to mildew, a flopping habit, or washed-out flower color, all because we love the person who gave it to us. Old-fashioned iris seems a bit dowdy compared to modern hybrids, but they're often passed along by friends and families and even from generation to generation. Many of my iris, admittedly dowdy, have been in my family for so long that their true names have long been forgotten. I know them as "Aunt Ida," "Aunt Ola," and so forth. I call them the dead relative iris. No doubt someday there'll be an "Uncle Rob."

"Pass along" plants have been traded over the garden fence since, well . . . since gardening began. These are the plants so well suited to cultivation under a wide variety of circumstances that they can easily be divided or rooted from cuttings, or that seed themselves freely. If you talk to some garden snobs, these are humble, insignificant plants, barely a cut above weeds. They're often branded as weedy or invasive. Under the right circumstances, almost any plant can be characterized this way. Given just the right soil and exposure, lots of plants grow exceedingly well. Those that overdo it get punished and branded as

*The brassy tone of bumblebee daisy (*Rudbeckia triloba*) calls for equally bold companions such as purple verbena and a scarlet cultivar of California poppy.*

not fit for a "proper" garden. To some snobs, only rare and hard-to-grow plants are worthy. That's nonsense.

I revel in the humble, undignified plants that truly want to grow in my garden. It's a healthy relationship, unlike the unrequited love I've felt for the rarities that would rather die than share my garden. Perhaps they died of embarrassment among the rogues gallery of self-sowers and aggressive spreaders.

On the other hand, if you give some plants an inch they will take a mile—literally. There's a single nonnative blueberry plant in New Zealand that reportedly has colonized a mile of beachfront property. With nothing to keep them in check, such as natural predators and diseases, strangers in a strange land can go berserk. Kudzu vine devours barns and water hyacinths clog waterways in the South. Bittersweet and ivy strangle trees along the Mid-Atlantic Coast and New England. Lythrum chokes out native plants in wet places throughout the northern tier of states, while tamarisk sucks streams of the West dry. And don't get me started on tumbleweeds, Russian thistle, yellow clover, bindweed, and dandelions. Would it really be too much trouble for my local parks department to spray the dandelions before they bloom? The seeds fall on my neighborhood like an infiltrating rain (I'm just a block from a park) and cause me many hours of work with my Japanese fisherman's knife. But I digress.

Some gift plants should be viewed with suspicion. They may be ideal for tough spots such as areas of dry shade or steep,

*Dark foliage adds depth to a garden, with red orach (*Atriplex hortensis *'Rubra') popping up artistically. I cut them to the ground in midsummer to regenerate and to prevent rampant seeding.*

sunny slopes. Given a cushier lifestyle, they may get way out of hand. The culprits vary from region to region, but some ornamentals that should be accepted warily include pink knotweed (*Polygonum capitatum*), bishop's weed or snow-on-the-mountain (*Aegopodium podagraria*), and creeping bellflower or cancer-of-the-garden (*Campanula rapunculoides*). These three will burrow under driveways to find new territory to conquer. World domination is seemingly part of their genetic codes. Every state has a list of noxious weeds: you may wish to consult with your county extension agency. Some plants that

*Airy sprays of tall verbena (*Verbena patagonica*) and black-eyed Susans—*
both self-sown—impart a loose, meadow feeling to the garden as the summer progresses.

made the noxious plant list don't, in my estimation, deserve to be on it. But it's worth staying informed.

Annual Art

Some control freaks can't stand the idea of plants deciding for themselves where they want to grow. Plants don't make an actual decision, of course, because that would presume they are capable of forming intent. Some do have the uncanny ability to sow themselves in just the right spot. The trick is to recognize that when you see it.

Self-sowing annuals help to fill in a budget garden quickly. They're to be treasured, even if they do need a bit of policing. Around the middle of April, I start my weekly rounds with my Japanese fisherman's knife, seeking out not only the stray dandelion that's hiding inside a clump of iris foliage, but the tiny seedlings of annuals sprouting all over the place. Some species come up as thick as dog's hair, while others just pop up hither and yon. What sows itself with abandon varies from region to region but for much of the country this often includes marigold, cosmos, sunflower, nasturtium, morning glory, black-eyed Susan, bachelor's button, tall verbena (*Verbena patagonica*), larkspur, Johnny-jump-up, and various poppies, such as California, corn, and bread seed poppies. Add to that list biennials such as money plant (*Lunaria annua*), foxglove, and dame's rocket (*Hesperis matronalis*).

These eager self-sowers are great annuals. Tough, tenacious, and drought-tolerant, they help the garden lose its

My big project for the summer, this new arbor made from old porch columns anchors the garden and ties in the flowering branches of the catalpa tree.

overdesigned look. When all plantings are spaced evenly in the beginning—as people usually do—nature steps in to soften our rigidity. I'm grateful for this. Larkspur makes an especially graceful addition to those big clumps of golden yarrow, maiden grass, and globe thistle at the back of the border. Cosmos and sunflowers belong back there too, mingling with hollyhocks and shrub roses. California poppies fill holes amid shorter perennials and have the knack of finding spots in cracks and near paving stones. Where conditions suit them, these brilliant annuals will germinate so thickly

People who make collages should be good at container groupings; I tend to move pots around when the spirit moves me.

and petunias, may indeed revert to forms closer to their original, wild forms when they sow themselves in the garden. Hybrids are the result of crossing two parent plants under controlled conditions. Several generations of crosses may go into creating new annual hybrids. It all unravels in the garden, when bees flit from flower to flower, undoing human control over the progeny. I like it when marigolds start to look more like the single-flowering wild plants of Mexico, or when petunias begin to resemble their sprawling, scented South American ancestors. They become more visually compatible with the perennials we grow.

Let's face it: most annuals are still bred for public park planting. They've become stumpy and dumpy. The emphasis on uniformity and compact form is a trend that's been going on since the Victorians first decided to display their wealth with elaborate floral carpets in the middle of their lawns. After all this time, I guess it's not just a trend but also an ingrained part of the way big seed companies do business. Surely they've come up with some terrific hybrid vegetables and annuals over time, but the dwarf race they've created isn't worth much to the average gardener. Though I've designed several formal public gardens where we created Victorianesque designs with these bedding annuals, their main use stops there. If you want to spell out your name or create a floral clock on your front lawn, be my guest. But if you're serious about creating a pretty garden, pass up the six-packs of overbred pygmies.

that none of them can thrive. That's where you step in, thinning them to at least 6 inches between plants. While it's a bit tricky, they can be dug and moved to other locations where they might be needed. Try not to bare-root them; leave as much soil as possible around the roots even when you dig up more than one seedling at a time. They can always be thinned again later once they've become re-established.

Self-sown annual flowers act like wildflowers, whether they're native or not. They possess a wildflower grace that the highly bred, six-pack annuals do not. Some hybrid annuals, such as marigolds

There simply aren't enough blue flowers to suit me. Cape plumbago, a tender South African shrub, contrasts with orange and yellow beautifully.

Blue foliage is equally effective in the garden, as the thin blades of blue fescue complement 'Homestead Purple' verbena, thyme, and catmint.

The easiest and least expensive way to add annual grace to your garden is to scatter seed. For a great number of them, the best time is fall, when nature is scattering them herself. Poppies, larkspur, and bachelor's button respond well, usually germinating in winter. Many perennials may also be sown this way, including blue flax, feverfew, meadow sage, and many others. This creates strong, husky plants that bloom early and vigorously. You can also sow them in winter or early spring, but don't wait too long. Seeds need to stay consistently moist for several weeks as they germinate and put down young roots. An afternoon of hot, dry wind can ruin them.

As you scatter the seeds, using a motion as if you're feeding chickens, go ahead and step on the seeds so they make firm contact with the soil. By the way, if you've never fed chickens, simply make rounded motions with your arms as you let the seeds slip through your fingers. Needless to say, a calm, still day works best, unless you're thinking your neighbor might like poppies. If you're working from a path, use a board to press the seeds in the soil. Bigger seeds such as nasturtium and sunflowers should be pushed into the soil with your thumb or forefinger to about a half-inch deep.

For new gardeners, the biggest obstacle to sowing from seed is distinguishing the good plants from the weeds. Some are really easy to identify, such as red orach with maroon seedlings or California poppy with lacy gray leaflets. In general, however, it takes practice to recognize which are the flowers and which have to go. Sometimes it's best to become acquainted with the weed seedlings first—whatever is common to your area—and go after them. With a bit of luck, what remains are the flowers you scattered.

In some areas, and for some annuals, it's best to start them early inside and transplant them into the garden or containers later. These are usually the heat-loving tropical flowers that take their time to get going. If you live in a warm, humid area, this usually doesn't present a problem. My sister in Florida has no trouble with many annuals and vegetables that she sows directly in the ground, such as tomatoes, peppers, eggplant, salvia, zinnias, flowering tobacco, and impatiens. On the other hand, these would never get up to speed in my Colorado garden. I need to give them a headstart inside, then transfer them outside when the weather stays dependably warm at night.

Although I sometimes plan ahead where certain annuals should be planted (such as moss rose along my garden path), usually I wing it. I wander around with seeds, hoping inspiration will strike. Mealycup sage (*Salvia farinacea*), in either its blue or white form, blends in almost effortlessly with almost anything else. Pretty, fragrant 'First Love' dianthus complements pale yellow yarrow or blue catmint with its single, pink flowers. *Nicotiana langsdorffii*, an odd flowering tobacco with dangling, chartreuse bells on stems up to 3 feet tall, consorts beautifully with almost any other flower, be they pastel or primary colors. Zinnias, to my mind, look their best against ornamental grasses, which tend to counteract the zinnias' stiff growth habit. The new kinds of zinnias, such as 'White Star', are bred from the species *Z. angustifolia*, which has a natural rounding, trailing form and single flowers. They're the opposite of the standard upright types and look pretty when spilling from pots or cozying up to larger perennials.

One thing about zinnias: they're really best displayed in groupings of a single color. By all means use the color mixtures in the cutting garden or vegetable garden—where the primary objective is picking—but they're kind of a mess as a mix. Most annuals look best in solid colors, otherwise the effect is of confetti confusion. I'm guilty of planting mixed moss roses along my path last summer, only because it was an afterthought to get them in the first place, and I waited so long the single color mixes were sold. I won't let that happen again. Although I enjoyed them thoroughly (What else could I do?), it was just too frantically cheerful. This season I'm shopping early

In the forlorn strip between the street and sidewalk that westerners call the "hellstrip,"
I've replaced the gravel laid by the previous owners with a mixture of tough flowers
such as black-eyed Susan, penstemon, and snow daisy.

for 'Sundial Mango' or another of those sherbet shades that go with nearly everything. The reason I need to buy a flat is that I've never had a particular knack with growing these simple annuals from seed. It happens.

Urban Sprawl

Annuals that cover ground quickly can be a boon to gardeners with big spaces to fill. The batch of plants we grow as annuals, but that are really mostly tropical perennials, includes the trailers and sprawlers. Some can easily cover a couple of square feet during the summer or make containers seem lush and overflowing in a stylish way. They can also drape over retaining walls or carpet a slope.

The best of these sprawling plants include sweet potato vines, licorice plant, lantana, wishbone flower (*Torenia fournieri*), Cape plumbago, verbena, sweet alyssum, the recent 'Wave' series of petunias, purple heart (*Tradescantia pallida* 'Purple Heart'), and wandering Jew. They can usually be purchased in small pots, customarily the 4-inch size, at a nominal cost considering the ultimate size they can attain. If you have indoor winter facilities, most can be easily propagated from cuttings.

Except in very cool summer areas, most people do quite well with sweet potato vines. They start small, with just a few golden-green or deep bronze leaves on a plant hardly big enough to be called a vine. With water, heat, and food, the plants grow nearly as fast as the proverbial magic beans, rolling out streamers of ornamental foliage. Often

Primary colors of red yarrow, blue bachelor's buttons, and black-eyed Susan thrive in my hellstrip with little care.

used solely for containers and hanging baskets, sweet potato vines can also be extremely effective planted at the front of a border, romping through plantings like a rambunctious golden retriever. They're very nice with shorter ornamental grasses, cannas, and asters. Sweet potato foliage breaks up a monotony of plain green and contrasts in very different ways, depending on whether you use either the golden or bronze forms.

One of the best basket plants, licorice plant (*Helichrysum petiolare*) neither looks nor smells like licorice. I can only assume there's a distant cousin in its family that has something to do with flavoring candy. At any rate, licorice plant sprawls perfectly; its feltlike, silvery, round leaves are lovely in conjunction with any number of flowers such as lobelia, ivy-leaf geraniums, verbenas, million bells (*Callibrachoa*), petunias, and twinspur (*Diascia barberae*). The variety of licorice plant called 'Limelight' offers a slight variation, with very pale, sea foam green leaves, while a variegated form looks like a combination of 'Limelight' and the standard silver form. All are great, with the one caveat that in torrid weather, the stems and leaves near the plant's center may blacken and "melt out."

Lantana has become a southern standard, but this pretty trailer can also be used in many different regions except the very coolest. The common orange and red form may not suit everyone's taste, so look for lavender, pink, and yellow forms. A pretty bright yellow cultivar features green leaves edged in gold. Once again, while they make good container plants, lantanas also can be used as fast-growing ground covers. I once used the lavender form to spill over a retaining wall of buff-colored sandstone to good effect.

Wishbone flower used to be represented by an upright little annual suitable for growing in places where you'd plant impatiens. 'Summer Wave' changed all that. These fast-growing heat lovers from Southeast Asia have become ideal candidates for hanging baskets, adding the bright blue flowers that so effectively contrast pinks, yellows, and grays. 'Summer Wave' makes a good replace-ment for lobelias in areas where summer heat spoils them.

South African Cape plumbago (*Plumbago auriculata*) is often seen as a landscape shrub on the West Coast, but I use it in pots. I save the plants from year to year, cutting them back rather haphazardly in midwinter to tighten them up. Then I set them outside in late spring and let them sprawl, which they do effortlessly, producing endless clusters of powder blue, five-petaled flowers resembling those of phlox. That clear, pale blue is a bit unusual and especially beautiful combined with pink flowers, so these pretty shrubs are well worth saving each season.

Most gardeners are no strangers to verbenas, sweet alyssum, and petunias. I must admit I avoided them for years. I had problems with performance and predictability. Now I'm planting them again, thanks to improved varieties. Standard verbenas were the spider mite magnets of my garden, so I gave them up. The improved sorts, grown from cuttings rather than seed, grow and bloom with abandon. I like the designer colors such as deep plum, crimson, and coral pink, all suitable for pots and baskets, but especially ideal at the front of a bed or border to spill onto a path. Sweet alyssum can be used the same way, but is more often seen lined up in rows. I like it in a loose way (as it often seeds itself) and in containers, but mainly for its wonderful fragrance of honey on a warm day. The 'Wave' petunias, in colors of purple, pink, and white, might bring other gardeners back to these badly used and abused plants. They can cover ground quickly and

Like a frame around a picture, these sidewalk plantings enhance the garden far better than strips of lawn could. They use far less water as well.

prettily, and of course they can create monstrous baskets. Mix them in with some contrasting foliage—sweet potatoes, licorice plant, and the like—since petunia foliage still isn't much to write home about.

Speaking of foliage, a few other trailers deserve mention. Purple heart has super foliage—more purple than that of the dark sweet potatoes—and makes other plants look grand, especially those with pastel flowers and silver leaves. It has flowers of its own—clustered in its leaf axils—in a pleasant shade of violet pink. Purple heart is also great with bright coleus. The purple and silver-metallic form of wandering Jew (*Tradescantia zebrina*), sometimes called silver inch plant, makes another super accent plant, in shade or partial sun, to complement purple, lavender, and white flowers. The very easiest of plants to grow (just break off a piece and stuff it in some soil), purple heart and wandering Jew can help fill baskets and pots for no cost at all. In areas where frost never threatens, they can also be used as shady ground covers.

"Hellstrips" Are for Heroes

Though it's largely a phenomenon in western states, the concept of converting the area between the sidewalk and street into a water-wise flower garden is taking

*In a portion of the hellstrip, native lavender fleabane daisy (*Erigeron speciosa)
makes a fine partner for the ever-present snow daisies.

hold across the country. This hot, dry strip of property—hence the nickname "hell-strip"—remains one of the most difficult areas to maintain, especially if it's covered in lawn. Trapped between concrete on one side and asphalt on the other, the grass is usually compacted and stressed. Water often runs off instead of soaking in, trickling down the gutter into storm drains, carrying pesticides and fertilizer salts.

It takes courage to buck convention and try a new concept. With recent western droughts, it makes more sense than ever to replace water-guzzling turf with perennials that actually thrive in hot, dry conditions. Municipal ordinances or homeowner associations covenants may dictate what you can or cannot plant in this area, which is usually owned by the city or town—but with the responsi-bility of maintenance left to you. I've always thought the time and labor lavished on these forlorn strips was largely wasted.

I planted one of the very first hellstrips twenty years ago. Since then, I've converted these areas to flowers in both of my subsequent gardens, including the present one. It was a bit more of a challenge this time since I live on a corner lot. While I was working on it initially, removing a black plastic liner and gravel coating placed by the previous owners to save water (not a success), it seemed like miles of hell.

Using gravel in this manner doesn't make sense either. While it may cut your water usage, it will add to the heating around your home, requiring extra electricity for cooling, which is generated by water. Did I mention it's ugly?

Let's talk pretty instead. In the unique urban and suburban environments where hellstrips exist, the flowers that will thrive there may vary a bit from region to region. The idea is to find drought-tolerant, resilient low-growers. I'm constricted somewhat by a city ordinance that says nothing can be taller than eight inches (I bend the rules a little bit). I've had the weed police pay me a visit (tipped off by a neighbor, no doubt, who preferred the gravel) but I made my case for drought-tolerant natives and adaptable perennials. In a follow-up appointment, they were really impressed with the flowering little meadow that sprang up. Well, it didn't just spring up.

After removing the gravel in fall, I waited until spring to start planting. I used seedlings from my borders (which are also drought-tolerant) and started moving them in late March. This took several weeks. I scattered seeds of poppies, bachelor's buttons, and blue flax. I thought I had it made until seeds I hadn't planted started to appear. I waged battle with zillions of weed seeds. That lasted through June, but in the meantime the plants I had chosen grew quickly and started to really look like something. I added store-bought seedlings such as ice plants, Mediterranean pinks (*Saponaria*

Rob's Hellions

Artemesia 'Silver Mound'	Mexican evening sunrose
Basket-of-gold	Oriental poppy
Black-eyed Susan	Penstemon
Blue flax	Potentilla 'Miss Wilmott'
California poppy	Prairie smoke
Callirhoe	Prickly poppy
Catmint	Rudbeckia 'Goldsturm'
Colchicum	Saponaria
Creeping phlox	Sedum 'Voodoo'
Cupid's dart	Siberian squills
Dianthus	Snow daisy
Dwarf baby's breath	Sun drops
Fleabane daisy	Tall verbena (talk about bending the rules)
Grape hyacinth	
Hen and chicks	Thyme
Indian blanket	Yarrow
Iris	Yucca
Lavender	And an assortment of strays
Mat daisy	
Meadow sage	

ocymoides), dianthus, thyme and Mount Atlas daisy from my favorite nursery. All told, I spent less than a hundred dollars to plant 180 by 6 feet of hellstrip.

The challenge in transforming a hellstrip is to create interesting combinations of plants that capture your attention as you stroll down the sidewalk. The advantage of using many of the same

Geraniums would fry by lunchtime in these little pots, but handsome succulents take neglectful watering in stride.

species over and over is that, from across the street and down the block, there's a nice harmonious froth. I'm quite pleased with the way this planting frames my picket fence and the garden within it. Almost every plant has survived and grown, woven together into an ever-changing tapestry with a long season of interest.

When Strays Arrive

It happens all the time to most gardeners. A friend or relative brings us a hunk of some perennial or a cutting, or perhaps we find a one-of-a-kind at the nursery at an end-of-season jumble sale. What do you do with just one? It's fine if it's a tree or shrub since it's perfectly logical that you need just one crabapple or lilac bush. But how do you work in just one thing, especially if strays keep arriving? It's difficult to make a pleasing design from drifts of one.

When strays arrive, there are two ways to handle it. The first option is to make a holding bed. In an inconspicuous spot—perhaps as part of the vegetable or cutting garden, or even tucked behind the garage—create a spot for the strays. With some care, they'll likely increase in size so that they'll eventually be big enough to divide into several pieces. If you can get at least three pieces to transplant, you've got a drift.

The other option is to showcase the one plant against a substantial drift of something else. For example, say someone gives you a single lady's mantle plant. If you've got a whole bunch of catmint (like I do), snuggle the lady's mantle up to the catmint, where its chartreuse flowers and pretty, dew-catching leaves will sparkle next to the fuzzy haze of lavender-blue catmint. Then stuff a whole bunch of 'Dragon's Blood' sedum or something with similar contrasting foliage as a skirt for the lady's mantle. You've suddenly made a castoff into a focal point.

Handsome Herbs

Many of my super-chef friends put me to shame with their breads and pastries, but I've got a knack for cooking with herbs.

One of the pleasures of grooming plants is the fragrance. Lavender and scented geraniums provide contrast for a variegated pineapple and—once again—'Red Dragon' begonia.

My secret? I grow my own fresh herbs. I also rely on ambience and alcohol to glaze over any shortcomings in a meal, but that's another story. I'm quite proud of my salmon with fennel, rosemary chicken, and tuna salad with tarragon. And a salad just isn't the same without dill, basil, or edible flowers such as violets, chives, and sunflower petals.

Growing herbs isn't just about spicing up your cuisine, it's more of a way of living. One definition of herbs is the "useful plants," whether you put them to use in the kitchen, linen closet, bathtub, or medicine chest. I rely on a number of useful plants throughout my house and garden. Bundles of santolina hang in my closet to protect my sweaters and sports coats from moths. I keep a pot of *Aloe vera* handy for those inevitable kitchen burns and yellowjacket bites; just break a fleshy leaf in half and dab on the soothing sap. My sheets and pillowcases smell sweetly of lavender. It's said to promote a good night's sleep. I know a woman who stuffed fresh lavender into her insomniac husband's pillow. The desired effect never occurred, as he tossed and turned all night, finally bellowing, "What are these sticks doing in my pillow!" or words to that effect.

Aromatic herbs make work in the garden more stimulating. I brush up against them as I work, each one triggering an olfactory memory or sensation. Artemisia reminds me of driving on I-25 near Pueblo after a thunderstorm, with the bracing scent flooding the cab of my pickup and lightning bolts flashing vividly over the eastern plains. Transplanting some lemon thyme last week, I became overwhelmingly thirsty for a glass of iced tea. Lavender, perhaps the most popular of all the aromatic herbs, reminds me of the soap in my grandmother's bathroom, rose gardens in England—where the bushes look far lovelier with a skirt of lavender—and the sun-drenched hills of southern France that I long to see and smell again.

To trigger lavender memories of your own, scour a couple of nurseries. A number of hardy varieties can be found such as English lavender (*Lavandula angustifolia*), represented by deep purple-blue 'Hidcote' and paler 'Munstead', both named for famous English gardens. Tender varieties include fringed lavender (*L. dentata*), with finely dissected leaves and stems with multiple flower heads of pale blue flowers, and Spanish lavender (*L. stoechas*), a showy sort for container gardens with flower heads with rosy lavender petals sticking out the tops like feathers. Lavenders make classic companions for lilies, daisies, mallows, and, as mentioned, roses. In a dryland garden, try pairing them with penstemons, snow daisies, or lamb's ears.

The hardy varieties are easy to grow in a sunny location, but take care in clay soil as too much water can easily drown them. If you garden on a rooftop or balcony, don't hesitate to try any of the hardy sorts in planters or pots as they stand a good chance of making it through the winter. Potted tender lavenders also require sun and can be overwintered indoors in a sunny window or sunroom. Plant some this week for a sensory sensation.

Slate blue paint makes an effective foil for bright dahlias, begonias, diascia, New Zealand flax, flowering maple, strawflowers, and many pots of succulents. That's Rose wagging her tail.

Kid's Stuff

There's nothing truly magical about gardening. The results are pretty much predictable, depending on conditions. However, for children who may think that vegetables come in plastic bags from the supermarket, gardening seems like magic. Some of my earliest childhood memories are from my family's vegetable garden. I helped to plant—and also pick and squish tomato hornworms. There's a funny family photo in the garden with my sister and brothers and our sheepdog. With our overalls, missing teeth, and dirty faces, we look like characters from *The Grapes of Wrath.*

Perhaps your children are more photogenic. But part of the fun of gardening—at any age—is getting dirty. If they learn something and manage to grow some carrots or corn to eat, all the better. Kids learn by example, as I did, and by trying things on their own. A little patch of ground is enough, especially if it's marked off and belongs expressly to a budding gardener. I can tell you from experience that kids can share chores in their vegetable garden, but they need their separate patches of earth. Otherwise there will be turf wars over how many sunflowers versus radishes.

Most adult gardeners need almost instant gratification, so it's small wonder that kids need fast-growing, quick-producing plants. It helps if they also happen to like the taste. I like almost any vegetable, perhaps because I had a hand in growing the ones I was served as a boy. I'm not saying that gardening will make a picky eater suddenly learn to love squash and brussels sprouts, but vegetables taste better when you grow them yourself. Pulling the first radish, washing it off with the hose and biting in to it is one pleasure that never gets old. I graze in my garden quite often, eating fresh peas and cherry tomatoes right off the vine.

Gardening teaches us all to appreciate nature. When a child plants and tends a little plot of earth, he or she learns that results come from vigilance and patience. He learns that things don't always go as planned, and drought, hail, wind, and insects can play a part in growing plants. Not all bugs are bad: ladybugs eat pests like aphids and honeybees pollinate flowers and sting only as a last resort since they die afterward. And once a child has triumphantly raised a stand of zinnias or a peck of tomatoes, he'll understand what goes into every garden he sees or meal he eats. Mowing the lawn for allowance money doesn't seem to teach the same sort of lessons.

Some people feel they need to head to the mountains or beach to get in touch with nature. Nature is right in your own backyard. Earthworms wriggle in freshly spaded soil (and I always feel a pang of guilt when I cut one in half). Butterflies flutter over dill and verbenas. Finches hang upside-down to feast on the mammoth sunflowers you've grown for them.

Gardening connects children with a way of life most of our ancestors practiced until only recently. It's part of our nature to want to grow plants. Some of us are more inclined to take it to an extreme than others. I can't even imagine what my life would be like now

Most kids like to get dirty in the garden. My parents allowed me to experiment with plants at an early age. I'm still at it.

if I hadn't learned to garden at an early age. Even if your kids don't choose to become professional horticulturists, I suspect they'll at least eat better and have nice yards.

Container Crazy

I'm crazy about pots. I like them almost as much as the plants that live inside of them. Collecting them can be an anytime—but particularly off-season—pleasure for any gardener. Almost every pot I own has a story (I won't bore you with details), bringing back memories from vacations, thrift-store and tag-sale rummaging, and, of course, friends.

The most utilitarian of garden objects, pots serve several vital functions. First, they're home to plants we can't or don't want to grow directly in the ground (this includes houseplants). For people who garden in clay, container gardens offer a place for loose, friable soil that's more suitable for many plants that sulk and die in clay—things such as lilies, tomatoes, and lavender. At the other end of the spectrum, those of us who garden in sandy soil that retains moisture poorly, can easily formulate a growing medium for plants that prefer wet feet such as cannas, caladiums, and elephant's ears. For the drought-stricken West, container gardening affords a way to enjoy these moisture-loving beauties without violating water restrictions.

Secondly, pots beautify our homes and gardens. Outdoors, they and their contents serve as focal points and, clustered together, become oases of beauty on patios, decks, balconies, and roofs.

I've never seen a garden that had too many pots. That's easy for me to say since my enthusiasm for containers is tempered only by my budget. My main patio is full. So is my porch and bedroom balcony. The perennial border has a dozen rolled rim terra-cotta pots lining the path at 8-foot intervals. I tell myself these add substance and order amid the chaos. The vegetable garden is similarly structured, and I've finally resorted to gardening on the roof of my potting shed, where squash and nasturtiums spill down for picking from their planter boxes.

Each fall I go through the frenzied ritual of hauling my potted tropicals indoors, usually during the first snowstorm. That's when I'm most grateful for the plastic and fiberglass pots that host my biggest plants, such as angel's trumpets (*Brugmansia*) and palms. Even a decade ago, you'd never have found plastic or fiberglass on my patio. But manufacturers have made great strides in producing pots that closely mimic terra-cotta. You can always hide ugly pots at the back or in the middle of a grouping, or plan to cascade licorice plant or sweet potato vine down their sides. Even so, my favorite pots include the classic rolled-rim terra-cotta ones and the relatively new glazed ones. Most of the latter are imported from Malaysia and Vietnam and come in a rainbow of colors, from cobalt and black to turquoise, sage, forest green, buff, plum, and wine red. Did I leave any out? These colors invite creative combinations. Chartreuse sweet potato foliage appears particularly vibrant against the turquoise and cobalt pots I use.

Glazed pots first started appearing at garden centers about a decade ago. But long before that—in the '40s and '50s—pretty little glazed pots were used by African violet fanciers. Made by American ceramics companies like McCoy, Shawnee, and Weller, these original little gems can still be found occasionally at flea markets and garage sales, as well as at antique stores, where you'll pay a premium. I first made my acquaintance with them through a friend with a house teeming with African violets. She had dozens of these pots (distinguished by their attached saucer design) and, like any nutty collector, wanted more. I promised if I found more in her favorite colors—pink, ivory, and yellow—I'd pass them on. I found quite a few in these colors for her, as well as in colors I liked, such as olive, turquoise, deep green, and celery. I decided my few African violets might prosper in them, like hers. They did, but I was becoming infatuated with succulents and decided they'd look even better in the colorful miniature pottery. The violets went by the wayside.

The great thing about succulents (and cactus, on which I also dote) is that they can live in very small pots for a very long time. A pot collector can't very well drag home a big container from his travels on a plane, but he can manage a few small pots in his carry-on. While puttering with my succulents and cactus, I can reminisce about trips to London, Nice, or Cancun. Few vacation mementos are put to such good use.

There seems to be a pot for every kind of taste. A friend collects animal pots. She has a barnyard of pots shaped like chickens, goats, pigs, bunnies, ducks, and every other critter you can imagine. As individual pieces, I find them too sweet and precious, but grouped on her flagstone patio and retaining wall and planted with hen and chicks and moss roses, they're quite appealing.

Finding the right pot for a plant (or vice versa) is the challenge. Rock gardeners—

Lots of Pots

TERRA-COTTA—the classic pot for almost every style and checkbook; a healthy growing environment, because the porous walls "breathe," allowing a transfer of water and air.

GLAZED CERAMIC POTS—retain moisture better than terra-cotta because the walls are nonporous; the glaze color can complement or contrast with the contents.

PLASTIC AND FIBERGLASS—formerly on the nondesirable list because of their ugliness, these types are now better designed, lightweight, and durable.

STONE AND ARTIFICIAL STONE—beautiful and extremely durable, these pots double as statuary, with a price tag to match.

CONCRETE—also durable and decorative, becoming more beautiful as they age, with moss and lichen colonizing the walls.

HYPERTUFA TROUGHS—the rock gardeners' delight, they are formulated from concrete, peat moss, and perlite. They simulate old stone sinks that became fashionable in England for containing alpines and succulents.

WOOD—tubs, barrels, and planters constructed of wood have the advantage of keeping soil temperature fluctuation at a minimum; the best choice for small trees, shrubs, and perennials to winter over in cold winter climates.

African violet pots from the '50s look great planted with small cactus and succulents.

METAL—cast-iron, aluminum, copper, and steel containers run the gamut from Victorian urns to sleek ultramodern planters; small ones can cook their contents quickly on sunny days.

or people like me who like rock garden plants but don't have any rocks—construct troughs from cement, peat moss, and perlite, reinforced by chicken wire or fiberglass strips. I used aluminum mixing bowls and cat litter trays as molds for mine. They're delightful. I don't own any stone pots—even artificial ones—or cement containers either, but I've used a number of them in gardens I've designed. Stone and artificial stone pots are lifetime investments. They're beautiful with or without plants—more like garden statuary. Needless to say they're extremely heavy. Equally heavy but more affordable are the cement containers, which look best as they age and become encrusted with lichen and moss.

Speaking of which, there are two schools of thought on mossy pots. In dry, sunny Denver, my pots remain moss-less, so my opinion really doesn't count. A new line of pots has moss imbedded in the clay. All you do is add water. I doubt they could withstand hot days with single-digit humidity, so I'm likely to remain on the outside of this debate. One thing I never fuss about is the buildup of fertilizer salts on terra-cotta. Some people soak and scrub; the most I ever do is run them through the dishwasher. The patina of an old, encrusted clay pot is beautiful to me, perhaps because it speaks of tradition and gardens of the past. In spring I soak empty pots in the sink or big garbage can before planting. Dry pots can wick moisture from both soil and roots. You'd be surprised how much they can "drink." Submerge them until the "champagne bubbles" cease.

In the meantime, most of my pots sit empty and upside-down in the cold. If you live in a cold winter climate as well, might I suggest that you employ a few for winter decoration? After you empty the soil, add coarse sand and create an arrangement of dried flowers, branches, and grasses. These freeze-dried bouquets will last for many months, until we can fill them up with living plants again.

Designing Dry

Good design is good design. It transcends regions, seasons, and even drought. Water restrictions don't necessarily affect the design of a garden; they only dictate the palette of plants from which to select. If you garden in the West and your garden has a stopgap, "just waiting for the drought to end" appearance about it, the time has come for a reality check. Sure, maybe next year could be a snowy one in the mountains, bringing more water the coming spring. But in the long run, a water-smart garden makes good sense. It can be as beautiful and sophisticated as any water-guzzling landscape and is more in tune with our natural surroundings.

Many of our sensibilities about garden beauty are based on an English model. It's a good one. They've got that border thing down. It's certainly influenced my work and translates well when we use climate-appropriate plants. The English border, however billowing and lovely, still has a couple of shortcomings. Fashioned to peak in June, it's usually dismal by fall and disastrous in winter.

A dry climate can work to the advantage of western gardeners, in that we have plenty of choices of late bloomers as well as plants that look great in fall and winter. Even so, most of us put the bulk of our efforts into the spring and summer garden, with off-season considerations secondary.

So it's summer—and what have we got? There's a haze in my garden, even on the sunniest day. The British work from a green base tone, whereas a xeriscape starts with silvers, grays, sage green, blues, and blue-greens. Heat- and drought-tolerant plants from around the world have often evolved with gray or sage green leaves— the better to reflect light rather than absorb it the way that deep green does—as well as fine hairs that further reflect and deflect. Lamb's ears, mulleins, horehounds (*Ballota* and *Marrubium*), partridge feather, Mt. Atlas daisy, thyme, and sea kale shimmer. The haze comes from the blue and lavender flowers above the gray and silver foliage. Catmints, Russian sage, blue mist spirea, meadow sage, German statice, lavender, and sea holly establish a starting point for any color scheme, whether you have a penchant for pastels or a bent for bold tones.

In a water-smart garden, there need be no shortage of colorful flowers, both annual and perennial, from spring till frost. My new garden puts the emphasis on jewel tones. The colors really pop against the blue and lavender haze. The hot pinks and magentas of rose campion, dianthus, Jupiter's beard, owl clover, agastache, purple coneflower, lavatera, purple ice plant, and wine cup show best—to my mind—against silvers and blues. Add some dashes of yellow—sunroses, wild zinnia,

yellow ice plant, 'Moonshine' yarrow, and silver mullein (*Verbascum bombyciferum* 'Arctic Summer'). Mix in some deep blue and purple for extra drama, such as larkspur, 'May Night' salvia, iris, and butterfly bush, and you have created my favorite color combination. It needs only one extra bit of color—chartreuse— to really send it through the roof. That's a tough commodity to find in the xeric palette, but ponytail grass (*Stipa tenuissima*) fits the bill.

Speaking of grasses, the shapes and textures of plants are of equal importance to color and insure interest in fall and winter. Grasses usually create fountain shapes. So do Russian sage, yarrow, butterfly bush, and agastache. They break up the roundy-moundy shapes of so many water-smart plants such as dianthus, tunic flower, meadow and garden sages, as well as creepers such as Mt. Atlas daisy, thyme, ice plants, sunroses, creeping phlox, soapwort, wine cup, and many kinds of sedum. While a tapestry of these ground-hugging perennials can be used effectively, rockets of hollyhocks, penstemons, mulleins, iris, and yucca, as well as airy flowers such as gaura, baby's breath, snow daisy, and blue flax can invigorate the flatness.

The juxtapositioning of varied textures creates greater interest in a water-smart garden, as well as distinguishing it from other creations in different climates. Although a majority of plants grown in dry regions display fine textures and smaller leaves (another adaptation from evolving in low-water situations) there are notable exceptions that have bold shapes and foliage. Silver mullein, for example, forms a rosette of large, velvety gray leaves from which it sends up spectacular stalks in its second year, studded with lemon yellow flowers. Set amid any number of finer-textured perennials, it's sensational. Just give it room. Other bold plants that add a sculptural quality to the dryland garden are prickly pear cactus—well, any cactus really—and while we're at it, any form of yucca, or agave, or hen and chicks. The latter, members of the genus *Sempervivum* (which means "live forever") don't really have designer cachet, but they're remarkably effective when set next to stones and less substantial creepers such as sedums and thymes.

The most remarkable perennials for contrast must be the sea kales. *Crambe maritima* boasts extraordinarily beautiful foliage, looking like a designer cabbage as blue as turquoise with wavy edges and white flowers about a foot tall. Its giant cousin, *C. cordifolia*, looks as if the rhubarb is on steroids until its huge airy heads of baby's breath–like flowers, which crown the mass of foliage, are revealed. It can grow 4 or 5 feet tall, with an equal girth, so it adds amazing bulk to the border. If you ever need to move it, rent a backhoe to dig out the long taproot. Giant sea kale might as well be considered with the shrubs when we design since it takes up as much room as most.

I've been working backward, I suppose, or perhaps just front to back. In this last group, the shrubs (even though I've already mentioned some), are great shapes, textures, flowers, and all-season interest, from lilacs and shrub roses to rabbit brush and fern bush, as well as pines, junipers, and spruce.

And I almost forgot the annuals. But I think in terms of colors and shapes rather than how long a plant lives. I adore California poppies, desert bluebells, larkspur, verbenas (especially statuesque lavender *Verbena bonariensis*) and dozens more. The real problem with designing dry isn't a lack of choices; rather, it's deciding what to exclude. Get some good books on gardening—no matter from which climates—and study what makes each photo beautiful. Then look at your own enormous palette of plants. Choose wisely (then stuff it all in). Create the garden of your dreams. Drought problems—what drought?

Return of the Natives

It might seem logical to assume that any plant native to your region would grow like gangbusters in your garden. That's not always true. I can think of dozens of nonnative species, introduced from Asia or Europe, that outperform true wildflowers in many parts of the country. Growing wildflowers sounds terribly romantic but there's a great deal of confusion about them. Just because a seed comes in a packet labeled "wildflower" doesn't make it so. They may be pretty, but Queen Anne's lace, Shirley poppies, chicory, oxeye daisy, bachelor's buttons, soapwort, and many other flowers are actually aliens that have adapted to life in North America. They're considered "naturalized" wildflowers. When they become too well adapted, like kudzu, loosestrife, Japanese honeysuckle, tumbleweeds, oriental bittersweet, water hyacinth, dandelions, or tamarix, they become public enemies.

True wildflowers may be native to an entire region or to just one forest or valley. Some natives are nearly impossible to grow in cultivation. Others perform admirably under a wide range of conditions. Wildflowers from woodland and wetland habitats across the country often find city life too stressful. Growing natives successfully must be considered on a case-by-case basis. The most popular types of gardens for natives across the country are woodland, meadow, and prairie. What's most appropriate for your garden depends on both your regional flora and individual conditions. A shady garden—even if it's in the middle of Kansas—might be better suited to a woodland garden than a prairie one. My own hellstrips are really just "enhanced" prairie. They feature both nonnative plants and what would grow here naturally had my neighbors and I not arrived, such as penstemons, fleabane daisy, wine cup, yucca, prickly poppy, and grasses.

What's remarkable about the new interest in growing native species is that many gardeners have come to a new appreciation of the flora that surrounds them. It used to be that only gaudy dahlias, gladiolus, and petunias were considered garden-worthy; anything that might appear along the roadside must be a weed and therefore highly suspect. While it is true that highways are often lined with foreign weeds such as tumbleweeds, thistle, and knapweed, native species often display a subtle beauty and grace that many overbred garden staples lack.

What is a native? And what makes it a good addition to your garden? Flowers don't acknowledge state boundaries. Look at where a plant evolved and you'll get a better understanding of whether it might grow well for you. Consider its native habitat—soil, temperature extremes, and rainfall—to understand its needs and possibilities. Get a guidebook to the wildflowers of your region. Some wildflowers have become so beloved that they have come to symbolize the areas where they grow. Bluebonnets blaze in Texas and California poppies gild the Southwest. Columbines represent the Rocky Mountain region. Glowing orange butterfly weed and bright purple Kansas gayfeather have come to symbolize the Midwest, while New England has become synonymous with its asters and goldenrod. Farther south, Virginia celebrates its pretty bluebells and the Carolinas their yellow lupine (*Thermopsis villosa*). Louisiana lends its name to the gorgeous wetland iris. Ozark sundrops (*Oenothera macrocarpa*) light up the southern plains, and Oconee bells (*Shortia galacifolia*) illuminate the moist woods and stream banks of the Blue Ridge Mountains.

Gardeners almost everywhere enjoy the widely adapted natives of the Great Plains such as Indian blanket flower, blue flax, purple coneflower, wine cup, black-eyed Susan, Mexican hat, bee balm, and many ornamental grasses. Our all-Americans are truly a marvelous bunch. You can inspect them in person in regional preserves, national parks, and

Indian blanket flower (Gaillardia aristata) *grows wild throughout the Great Plains and performs admirably in any number of situations, such as my hot, dry hellstrip.*

botanic gardens and easily create a suitable habitat at your home for them.

Our enthusiasm for native wildflowers must be tempered by respect. Never dig plants from the wild; buy only nursery-grown stock. Our expanding human population threatens that of flowers as their habitats shrink. One of our loveliest and least-known wildflowers, the tulip poppy (*Eustoma grandiflora*), is found only in Colorado and now only in a few remaining (and secret) areas of the eastern plains. In an odd twist, this humble prairie dweller, an exquisite gem with cup-shaped blossoms with satiny purple petals, has become a staple of the cut-flower trade, gussied up in pink and white—even double forms. You can grow this gorgeous native annual in your own garden from nursery-propagated plants though, surprisingly, it can be a bit fussy, especially in transplanting. The tulip poppy symbolizes the wildflower world we should treasure.

Native plants, when removed from their wild habitat, don't always grow with the vigor one might expect. In my home state of Colorado, our beloved aspens and columbines, when removed from their mountain homes, suffer and sulk on the hot dry plains. Some natives, such as Indian paintbrush, are nearly impossible to grow in cultivation. On the other hand, blue spruce and potentilla—two more mountain dwellers—perform admirably under a wide range of conditions. Growing natives successfully must be considered on a case-by-case basis.

The wonderful thing about the interest in growing native species is that it helps broaden our narrow definition of beauty. Roses and lilies may come to mind when we speak of beautiful flowers, but now many other non-traditional flowers are also called beautiful That's terrific progress for our natives.

Chapter Four
Penny-Pinching

*G*ardening should not be a pastime just for the well heeled. It should be accessible to everyone who longs for a beautiful and productive garden. Ironically, victory gardens were grown in times of wartime scarcity to save money by producing supplementary vegetables. Today, creating a garden rich with beauty and edibles has become more of a luxury than a necessity.

Costs of plants, seeds, pots, and tools can make gardening an expensive hobby, but sweat and smarts can help you avoid some of the costs. Invest where you need to in key items and plants, but use your ingenuity to save money on containers and identifying labels.

You need buy dahlias and oleanders only once.
Keep them from year-to-year and propagate them.

Most of us regularly recycle bottles, newspapers, and plastic. Expand that practice into your garden, using recycled items for planters and tools, from cottage cheese containers and milk jugs to old sheets and panty hose. The most seemingly worthless discards of all—garden debris and vegetable crisper castoffs—may make the biggest contribution to the health and beauty of your garden.

Even high-ticket garden structures, from patios to pergolas, can become affordable by using your ingenuity and being willing to do part or all of the work.

Some projects may take several years to plan and finally complete. Evaluate and sharpen your skills. Learn what you're capable of and what you need help to accomplish. If you're a savvy shopper, you're already well on your way.

Making the Most of Sales

Sniffing out a bargain, knowing where and when to shop, and frequenting flea markets and yard sales are important skills for the shoestring gardener. Shopping in these ways is not about finding cheap stuff, it's about finding quality stuff at low prices. Ultimately, shopping wisely will enhance the results of your gardening talents.

Retail nurseries seldom offer unbelievably great deals. After all, they have a lot invested in their plants. At the right times of the year, however, you can find some bargains—if you're willing to wait. After the mad spring rush, nurseries calm down a bit. There comes a point when it's not worth their effort to keep watering most annuals and vegetables. Small, independent nurseries often have good markdowns in early summer and may be willing to haggle. In fall, nurseries also want to unload as many perennials, shrubs, and trees as possible so they won't have to maintain them over the winter. You may find a jumble of pots on sale as well. A bit later on—toward Christmas—they'll also discount an assortment of bulbs. This is my favorite sale. And, at slow times for them, you'll sometimes find marked-down tools and pots in the lag before new merchandise arrives.

Partnering with friends and family to place orders for quantity discounts can pay off. Many nursery and bulb catalogs offer discounts if you buy three rose bushes of the same kind or a hundred tulips rather than a dozen. I especially like ordering bulbs by mail as they ship easily in their dormant states. I've rarely had bad experiences with deliveries of any kinds of plants. Online and mail ordering has expanded our options far beyond what a single nursery could carry. If you have particular weaknesses for certain kinds of plants, these resources help you add to your collections easily.

I'm a firm believer in supporting local nurseries. They make it their business to know your climate and soil and to hire knowledgeable staff to advise you. Occasionally, it's worth checking out the big discount stores. While they may not have a clue about your climate—and often bring in wildly inappropriate plants for your region—they can be a good source for standard plants at good prices. I'm talking about palms, ferns, junipers, and that sort of thing.

I wish I had more time for yard sales and flea markets, because you never know what valuable things you'll find at them. Pots, wheelbarrows, tools, yard furniture, and found objects may be just around the next block. I sometimes see people on *Antiques Roadshow* who've made incredible finds at tag and estate sales. These sales weren't in my neighborhood. Still, I'm pleased with some clay pots, tools, and chairs I've gotten this way.

Joining a plant society will put you in touch with people who are just as nuts about certain plants as you. If your passion is rock garden plants, daylilies, African violets, hardy plants, lilies, cactus and succulents, orchids, or dahlias, there's a group for you. Local gardening clubs will also connect you with a plant-minded community. Sharing is a way of life for these gardeners, unless it's one of the clubs that's really more about status and Louis Vuitton bags than statice and burlap bags.

Investment Plants

Not every plant can reasonably be grown from seed, struck from a cutting, or

The roses were a bonus when I bought the place, clustered over by the former garage.
I moved them to frame the view.

coerced from a friend. You'll just have to buy them. That doesn't mean you can't find them on sale, or buy younger, less expensive plants. When it comes to trees, many shrubs and some tropicals, annuals, and vines, you'll need to invest in them.

Let's start with trees. Most of us don't get an opportunity to plant many trees during our lifetimes. A house with an established landscape may come with mature trees. You may not care for the choice the previous owners made—or the placement—so it's usually a matter of making the best of what's there. In a new landscape, a blank slate, there's an opportunity to plant a half dozen trees or

so—depending on the size of the property. Make the most of it by reading up on the best and most beautiful varieties for your region. If you have room for more than a half dozen or so trees, you own a compound! Even on the odd chance that you're a really thrifty person of untold wealth, you can still follow my advice not to buy the biggest trees you can afford.

Smaller trees transplant so much better than larger ones that I don't recommend that anyone should buy big. While they try to support their top growth and put down new roots—or regenerate their severed roots—large trees simply sit without changing, sometimes for years. Younger versions adapt to their new soils and conditions much more quickly and will often catch up to and even surpass the once-larger trees. After a decade, you won't know which one cost $50 and which one cost $300.

Although a few people have the patience to grow roses and other shrubs from cuttings, I'm not acquainted with any. Younger, smaller shrubs catch up to bigger, more expensive ones just the way trees do. You can often find gallon pots at reasonable prices of such diverse shrubs as roses, blue mist spirea, barberry, azalea, rhododendron, hydrangea, euonymus, sumac, lilacs, and juniper. The same goes for vines such as grapes, clematis, wisteria, and honeysuckle. Patient nursery people have grown these from seed or cuttings expertly, saving us several fretful years of nursing them.

Believe it or not, I have grown peony species from seed. However, it took a very long time for them to flower. Those I grew in this way are pretty in a wild sort of way, but I wouldn't recommend this path to anyone but the nuttiest collector. To plant the peonies that we all love and cherish, just buy them. Some plants are known to be well over a century old, so this is truly an investment. I love tree peonies, too. They're a bit pricey (tree peonies are slow growers), but given proper placement and care, they'll live very long lives as well.

By and large, try to avoid transplanting trees, shrubs, roses, perennial vines, peonies, and tree peonies. Make a decision on placement and stick to it. Everything else, however, is movable,

removable, and potentially transient. I don't advocate moving perennials around every season. They'll object to this, especially taprooted perennials. And you want to take special care of named varieties for which you paid full price.

Named varieties of perennials such as *Coreopsis* 'Crème Brûlée' or *Gaillardia* 'Summer Kiss', which are grown from cuttings or division, can't be grown from seed by home gardeners. They are "sports" of perennials that exhibited some new, desirable characteristic such as variegated leaves, bigger flowers, different colored flowers than the norm, taller or more compact growth, or some other unusual trait. These named varieties can only be purchased. Once you have one, of course, you can make more by division. Some are patented, however, and if you decide to start your own little corner nursery, you're prohibited from propagating it.

Tropical plants are a slightly different story. The term "tropical" is relative, by the way. If you live in the Deep South or parts of California, they're not tropicals, but rather everyday plants you can buy anywhere. For the rest of us, they're exotic wonders that we grow on our summer patios and protect indoors during the winter. Some can be propagated from cuttings at home, but the initial plants need to be purchased. Some named varieties, like perennials, are sports with unusual characteristics. A good source for these (unless you've got a trip planned to California soon) is the mail-order trade. You'll get relatively small plants by mail but, in time, they'll fulfill their promise.

Potting Soil and Compost

Who'd have thought a century ago that people would pay for dirt one day? The expense of potting soil and soil amendments can really add up. Some experts advise not reusing potting soil after the first season, because there's the risk of a build-up of pathogens in the soil. From this, I can only assume that pathogens are really bad creepy-crawlers. I can further assume that a potting soil manufacturer's publicist first pointed out this possible danger. All I can say is, "Get serious." Soil has been reused since people first started growing plants. To think that soil becomes unsafe for plants after a single season is ludicrous. Soil itself is very old, composed of weathered rocks and minerals and all the plants that have grown in it, as well as all the animals that have once lived in it, walked on it, and eaten the plants that have sprung from it. We say "dust to dust" for good reason.

If something were to have gone horribly wrong in a container—perhaps tarantulas were nesting in it—I suppose I'd dispose of it. But I'm having a difficult time actually picturing something going wrong except for underwatering or overwatering that resulted in the death of the soil. Potting soil is one of the most important things to recycle in the garden. By investing in keeping it healthy—adding nutritious compost continuously—it will continue to sustain your containerized plants from year to year.

The contents of pots that I don't save for the winter get dumped into a big pile after they've been blackened by frost. The leaves, stems, and roots of the dead plants start to break down, even in winter. I burrow through the pile in late spring and take out the big chunks. Most of these will go into the compost pile. The rest is spaded and turned and mixed with fresh compost and new store-bought soil as needed to make it stretch. For most big pots, I fill the bottom third of the pot with some of the big chunks as well as half-rotted tree leaves. Then I put the soil on top and plant. The big stuff at the bottom will break down over the course of the summer, nourishing the plants as they do. This is really just composting in place. Please avoid the common but bad idea that some people use to skimp on potting soil: don't fill the bottom of a pot with rocks or packing peanuts. Organic materials make much more sense.

Composting seems to intimidate people because it sounds complicated and smelly. It needn't be either. What comes from the earth should be returned to it. And I don't mean by way of the landfill. I compost in a haphazard way in a pile by my potting shed. The pile contains garden debris—everything green—and I even toss in old produce, tea bags, coffee grounds, and eggshells. Things I don't add to the pile are grass clippings, citrus, potatoes, and large branches that would take decades to decompose. Most green things decompose with very little odor, except grass, citrus, and potatoes. If aging produce stinks in your vegetable crisper, it'll stink in your compost pile.

If you're the tidy type, buy an efficient, practical compost barrel that you crank every so often, rolling the contents like a cement mixer. And there's plenty of good how-to information in books about how to construct a compost bin, when to turn the compost, all about airflow, how to add "activators," and all that stuff. My approach is much simpler. I have a pile. I throw stuff on it and let nature take its course. It's free. And it's easy. My plants are extremely healthy.

Use It Up, Wear It Out

I'm not wild about plastic. In fact, plastic garden decorations in fluorescent colors really distress me. They distract from the real decorations in the garden—the flowers. Black plastic is often used as a liner beneath gravel or mulch. The soil beneath it, once a living thing teaming with worms and microorganisms, becomes a dead, barren wasteland. Save the black plastic for Halloween. On the other hand, plastic pots do have certain advantages, though it takes imagination to compensate for their undesirable colors and finish. We'll get to that challenge shortly.

Having the tendency to be a pack rat isn't such a bad thing for gardeners. Saving some items totally unrelated to horticulture can be useful. Whether you want to mess with this or not is up to you. The drawback is that, if overused, plastic milk jugs and cottage cheese containers could make your garden resemble a recycling center.

Fee, Fi, Faux, Fum

The best bargains in containers are plastic. You can buy big pots at rock-bottom prices, and there's actually an advantage to them: their contents dry out more slowly than in conventional terra-cotta pots. However, they're often produced in unappealing colors; usually an unconvincing terra-cotta burnt orange, forest green, or white. I've yet to find a way to make the green ones acceptable, but the white and orange are workable. I have exactly three white plastic rectangular planters. They sit on the roof of my potting shed (space is tight) and I plant squash, cucumbers, and nasturtiums in them. The shed is blue with white trim, so the white doesn't bother me, especially when the squash gets rambunctious.

Now for those orange plastic pots. There were times when I wouldn't have been caught dead with a plastic pot on my patio. But the prices are too tempting and the conditions inside plastic are perfect for some of my favorite plants like cannas and dahlias. Now I just don't get caught. It's all about faux finish. This came to me when a friend called to tell me he spotted some big plastic pots for four bucks each at the dollar store by his house. I told him to get me ten. When he brought them over, I was slightly unnerved by their appearance. Not only were they shiny, orange plastic, but also they were shaped and ornamented like Greek urns, with fluted sides and a Greek key design around the top lip. "Yikes," I thought, wondering how to hide them among my good pots, perhaps with sweet potato vines billowing forth.

Instead, I remembered that there were lots of cans of old paint in the basement from the previous owners. Why I hadn't disposed of them I don't know, but I remembered the wall colors I'd covered up the past few years, such as the mint

Can you spot the plastic imposter pot from the dollar store? It's in the center of the foreground, transformed by a fabulous faux finish.

green bathroom and the mushroom living room. It was a treasure trove of insipid colors down there. With some mixing, I came up with a dirty eggplant shade for the undercoat. I applied this with a kitchen scrubber, sponging and smearing to cover all but about 20 percent of the orange plastic. Then I cautiously dabbed on the mint green—sparingly—and added just a few highlights of mushroom. My plastic pots miraculously turned into copper urns. The layering of the three colors of paint created a fantastic—albeit unintended—verdigris finish.

Since then, I've used the same process to work magic on plastic pots of a plainer design. A dirtier green, with an undercoat of brown, makes me believe the pots have sprouted moss. (Rolling them in dirt and kitty litter helps the illusion.) Little highlights of tan and beige (perhaps from a blah bedroom) imitate the fertilizer salts that accumulate on real clay pots. Before you grab a sponge and some old paint, study your seasoned clay pots to see how they've aged over time. They're quite varied and wonderful. Try to imitate the subtleties of aged terra-cotta as you work.

Hardware and paint stores also sell sprays with textural finishes that can dress up clay pots. I've used ones that mimic sandstone and granite. It's best not to achieve the exact finish the can promises since it's usually too perfect. Use these sprays on top of each other and with sponging and smearing to get the instant look of age you like.

For aesthetic reasons, I still prefer the classic, rolled-rim terra-cotta pots. Put these classics in places of prominence with your faux creations tucked in inconspicuously. With proper care, clay pots last many years—especially if they're brought inside or emptied and stored for winter. But sometimes they crack. To extend their usefulness, take strong wire, encircle the pot just below the rim and twist with pliers until the wire is snug but not tight. I've seen this done on venerable old pots in the finest English gardens. It just adds to the charm.

Stuff We Throw Away

Unless it's disguised with a faux finish, you'll not find any plastic on display in my garden. It's carefully hidden away, used only for utilitarian purposes. There's a hoarding gene in my family (my mom was partial to margarine containers), so I've always been careful not to find anything plastic too useful. That said, I do use stuff in the garden that most people throw away. For example, men's cotton briefs—once the elastic is shot—can be shredded to make soft strips for tying up tomatoes and vines. (Dark colors are preferred over white.) Old T-shirts can be used in a similar manner. The best tying material, however, is old panty hose. It's soft and stretchy, perfect for tying a stem to a stake or trellis without injuring it. It's much better than anything you can buy commercially. Alas, I do not have a source. Yarn is also an inexpensive material for tying up what flops. Pick a dark olive, acrylic yarn, since wool won't last very long outside. I've had the same skein of yarn for almost a decade; it goes a long way.

I never throw away old blankets and sheets. I'm always worried about frost. Having a stockpile of bedding to quickly cover tender vegetation is a literal lifesaver. Keep bamboo stakes handy, too, so you can stick them around plants so

Rose inspects the altered patio landscape on the afternoon before the first forecast frost of the season, showcasing a decade of sheet selection.

that the weight of the wet sheets doesn't do as much damage as the frost or snow. In fall, my garden frequently resembles wash day in Calcutta. After use, I simply run the sheets through the drier, fold, store, and wait for the next threat.

For propagation, emptied plastic pots and six-packs are worth saving. When planting seeds, I reuse plastic six-packs, but I sterilize them first. I wash them out in a bucket to get rid of any clinging soil, and then I run them through the dishwasher. Alternatively, you could soak them in a solution of water and bleach. I also recycle plastic tags to label the seeds as they're sown. A visitor once asked me why the plants in my garden weren't labeled. Without attempting to be flip with her, I replied, "Because I know their names." But I'm a so-called expert who's been gardening for years. I should know the names. If you're a bit newer to gardening, don't feel bad if you haven't memorized all the names. But for heaven's sake, place that distracting tag at the back of the plant. In addition, consider making a map of your garden and put the tag info on it.

I'm loath to admit that I also save cottage cheese containers and film canisters to store seeds. I also hang onto netted mesh bags, like the ones oranges and avocados come in, for storing gladiolus and other bulbs over winter. Milk jugs can also be used outside as mini-greenhouses to give squash, pumpkins, and melons a jump start. Cut off the bottoms and set the jugs over the plants. Leave the caps off by day, but if it gets chilly at night, replace the caps. The interior can get very warm, so never leave the caps on during a sunny day. To shade newly planted seedlings from the hot sun, I sometimes use tomato support cages covered with newspaper held in place by clothespins. Needless to say, I never employ any of these tricks when guests are expected.

Structure and Style

Gardening remains one of the last bastions of exuberant personal style. In contrast, our clothes, hairstyles, and cars seem safe and dull. Quite frankly, I miss the style of the sixties and seventies when people dressed and drove with outrageous flair. Say what you will about minis, maxis, Mustangs, and microbuses, they weren't dull. Back in the day I drove an MGB and had a closetful of Saturday Night Fever styles. My current pickup and conservative sports coats pale by comparison. However, my garden reflects youthful expression that's mellowed with time.

Don't let convention dictate your garden's style. How many boring juniper and gravel landscapes dominate your neighborhood? Kick up your horticultural heels and make a bold statement. The architecture of your garden can be rustic, elegant, or whimsical. Every aspect of your design creates the garden's architectural signature, from the shapes of the

Things get a bit wild toward the end of the season, with morning glories, tall verbenas, and sunflowers disregarding all semblance of order.

Carpeted in catalpa blossoms, this rustic path imparts instant antiquity beneath the arbor built from old porch columns.

beds and borders to the outdoor furniture, arbors, and trellises.

I learned about style at an early age when my family moved to Loveland, Colorado. Our new neighbor across the street was the most passionate gardener I ever met. Her name was Katie Maser. Though I was only a third-grader, I spent nearly every waking minute with her in the garden and she became my best friend. Despite the fact I don't have any photos of it, I can still see every inch of that garden, from the red roses rambling over the front porch to living arches she made by tying and training two junipers together. Purple clematis cloaked an arbor

on the side of the house where we drank iced tea when we took a break from our gardening tasks.

From Katie, I learned how to stake plants, deadhead flowers, and plant seedlings in deep perennial borders. Her rose garden was a perfect five-pointed star carved in the middle of the lawn where I edged the grass and tried my hand at pruning. Flanking her driveway were two handled baskets, about four feet tall and as wide, formed from clipped junipers with pots of pink geraniums blooming within. Most kids my age dreamed of visiting Disneyland; I lived across the street from it.

With this early influence, it's small wonder I became a gardener. I still grow and treasure many of the plants that I first encountered in Katie's garden. I've decided just this moment that purple clematis is precisely what I'm planting to scramble up my patio arbor. I'm even imagining how a series of living juniper arches might add height and symmetry if positioned along my long garden path.

Paving Paths and Patios

One of the biggest wastes of space (to a gardener) is the automotive complex, i.e., the garage and driveway. While the neighbor across the street probably needs every square inch of his three-car garage for his collection of motorcycles, my needs are very different. My garage was too small for my truck and so contained all the stuff I never quite managed to rid myself of until one day last summer when I'd had enough. Later I'll relate how it turned into one of the most used rooms of my house. After the garage was transformed, there wasn't much point to having a driveway. It's gone too, transformed into a rustic path of recycled paving materials and extending beneath a long pergola. The conversion of the old driveway has added a charming, unexpected dimension to my garden.

I'm in no position to offer step-by-step instructions on how to lay a path or patio perfectly. Sure, I've done my fair share of paving projects in brick, flagstone, and concrete pavers, but I wouldn't submit them to *Handyman's Digest*. They're imperfect, but perfectly serviceable. If you've got energy, you can make a great path or patio. All you need is a wooden frame, builder's sand, a level, and a rubber mallet.

An existing concrete slab is the easiest surface to pave. It's already level. Enclose it in a wooden frame on the outside, fill with several inches of sand and have at it. Bricks are great for this. Use the mallet to keep them tightly packed next to one another and to "moosh" them firmly into the sand. Keep the level handy so you don't get high and low spots. If, however, you're paving over soil, excavate about 6 or 8 inches down, level the soil as well as possible, build the frame (it holds the pavers together and keeps them from shifting), lay down the sand, and have at it. I once laid a 12- by 12-foot patio the night before a tour group came to my garden. Scheduling a special event is a good motivator to get big projects done.

If I can lay a brick patio, so can you. My pets and I spend lots of time on the patio but Gruff really wants to go play in the garden.

Building centers often hold classes for do-it-yourselfers. Consider attending one about paving before you start.

Laying irregular stone takes a bit of creativity and more muscle. The pieces are larger and heavier than individual bricks. It's like putting together a jigsaw puzzle without the picture on the box. Just take it slowly and watch your fingers. Once you've laid bricks or concrete pavers, it's customary to sweep sand into the cracks. With flagstone or slate, it's better to put in soil so that the cracks can support low, creeping plants such as thyme. Some people prefer mortar between the stones to prevent plants from growing there. It's up to you. If you regularly use a snow shovel on a paved area in winter, skip the plants because you'll be scooping them off, too.

My latest paving projects, such as where my old driveway was, have been attempts in my garden to create "old" paths. I intersperse new pavers with recycled stones and bricks scrounged from alleys. I just keep adding to them as I get materials, so this is like piecing together a jigsaw puzzle—not only without the picture on the box but with some of the pieces missing. These paths, beneath my pergola and on the side of the house, remain works in progress. I don't worry about an even surface. I assure myself I'll be thrilled with the results as soon as plants colonize the spaces between the pieces. I like the feeling of instant antiquity, as if these old, crumbling paths have been here since long before me. Such creations, however, aren't very practical for dining patios or heavily trafficked areas such as

front walks. Chair legs and high heels are likely to get caught in the cracks.

The whole point is to imagine your paved spaces as you'd like them and then figure out how to make it happen. Living with a builder's concrete slab tacked onto the back of your house will stifle your creativity. Smash it, hide it, extend it, paint a mural on it, or make a mosaic of it. Similarly, don't settle for the silly winding path leading to the front door (which everybody cuts around anyway) that the previous owners thought would be lovely. While you may not think sledgehammering will be fun, you might discover how your aggressions just melt away as the concrete path disappears. After the hard work (keep hydrated and wear safety goggles), your muscles will be good and sore, but the pleasures of demolition are unexpectedly rewarding.

Up in the Air

Garden structures add much-needed vertical elements to the garden. A trellis, arbor, or pergola gets the garden off the ground and, let's face it, enables the keen gardener to squeeze in more clematis, morning glories, or climbing roses. Whether you buy or build these, make sure any structure is well anchored (usually in cement) and strong and tall enough to support whatever plants you select to grow on it.

In my case, I wanted a structure to enfold the garden on the edge of the property and add a strong presence. I already had several small trellises and arbors as accents and I had employed two of the old columns from my former porch to support an arbor attached to the garage. For my pergola, for which I drew inspiration from one I'd seen at an old funeral home, I stayed with the column theme. Since I had only one left, I searched the architectural salvage stores until I found a matching set of six. Then I found one more at an antique store.

Century-old columns come encrusted in many layers of paint. If you scrape and sand, be advised that you will encounter lead-based paint, so take precautions. I embraced the old patina of the columns and did a minimum of restoration. The concept of instant antiquity draws many gardeners to using recycled architectural elements. My friend Ed, a great carpenter, was dubious at first but soon warmed to my vision. It took me a day to dig holes for the concrete footing, and another for Ed to actually get the columns upright. My next-door neighbor came home that afternoon and yelled, "Hail, Caesar!" The columns definitely make a statement.

A network of beams and crosspieces tops the airy structure, which nestles beneath a venerable old catalpa tree. The catalpa, also sometimes known as the bean tree, is one of my very favorites for its large, heart-shaped leaves and beautiful, fragrant flowers in early summer. I'm really lucky to have such a great specimen growing on the property line and towering over my garden. The new pergola relates to the tree and, in turn, to the garden. It's quite pretty with the white catalpa blossoms that quickly fade under the July sun. I only managed to slap on a single coat of paint before I had to snap some photos.

Shady perennials are now thriving at its feet along my path of recycled brick, stone, and concrete and, as they knit together, will reinforce the impression that it has all been here for a long time. From the interior of my former garage, where I'm sitting as I write, it's a pretty view. One of my dogs is stretched out beneath the pergola in the cool shade. And I'm sitting comfortably on an old couch I found in the alley.

Summer Rooms, Work Spaces, and Potting Sheds

Perhaps you, too, will be inspired to install a pair of French doors in your garage and turn it into a summer room. Perhaps you'll just evaluate what you have and decide to turn a basically worthless storage space into something exciting and usable. After all, what are you storing in your garage or shed? Are you really going to use that exercise equipment or old carburetor again? Make the space work for you. I was surprised how much garden junk I had that I never, ever used. I got it down to the essentials and consolidated them in my potting shed. The latter was a Tuff Shed the previous owner erected behind the house near the alley. I painted it to tie it in with the other structures on my property and now it houses all the tools that used to be in the garage.

Today, my old garage feels like a beach house. Not one from Martha's Vineyard, to be sure, but it has a warm, inviting ambience. The contents are an eclectic mix, as if I'd rummaged through a tasteful granny's attic. Items came from alleys, garage sales, my basement, and

From this vantage point in the new summer room, Gruff can keep an eye on the garden. Most furnishings came from the alley.

building permit when I tore off and replaced my front porch, but not for the changes to my garage. You may or may not need permission to erect a shed. Arbors, trellises, and pergolas aren't generally considered structures by most municipalities and aren't covered by city codes but may be subject to other covenant restrictions. Walls and fences normally are subject to rules about their heights and placement as well. Thankfully, there are few restrictions on patios, paths, and raised beds, unless you live in a really strict community with a homeowners association with lots of restrictive powers, in which case you should probably just move.

Raised Beds Elevate Garden Performance

To get started in garden structures, try your hand at making a raised bed. It's a good place to build your confidence. Unfortunately, the image of the raised bed isn't always a good one. What comes to mind are dreary railroad ties piled several high, usually rotting and teetering precariously. Forget that. Raised beds not only serve a function, but also can be an important structural addition to your garden.

closeout sales at Hobby Lobby. My pets think I created this space especially for them. Cool on a hot day and comfy on a rainy one, the summer room provides them with views onto my two patios and beyond. They're alert for squirrels foolish enough to intrude or other neighborhood dogs on an outing with their owners. I like to read and write in this space, which blurs the distinction between house and garden.

When you build or remodel, check on codes in your city or county. I needed a

The need to create a raised bed stems from a common problem in many gardens: the soil may be unsuitable for what we wish to grow. Many vegetables, in particular, balk at putting their roots down in heavy clay or rocky soil. Many perennials and annuals also profit from being planted in an elevated bed filled with topsoil and compost. Steep slopes, where water runs off quickly, can be transformed from problem to perfection by building a series of terraced beds. Raised beds are proof against everything from poor drainage to careless drivers who flatten flowers that flank driveways. Gardeners with mobility challenges enjoy accessible gardening in raised beds as well.

Function, budget, and the architecture of your home dictate the choice of materials to construct a raised bed. There's nothing wrong with treated wood timbers, of course, but it may be wise in the long run to invest in stone, brick, or interlocking concrete blocks. I'm not especially fond of the looks of these block systems, but one of my neighbors grows sweet potato vines that cascade stunningly down the walls of her beds. For relatively low beds, dry-stacked stone walls (without mortar) are an option that you can do yourself. I've done a bit of dry stacking; it's laborious, but relatively easy once you get the hang of it. For walls taller than a foot or so, a professional mason should be called in to build the necessary concrete footing and achieve a straight, sturdy wall. When terracing a hillside, you'll also want to consult an expert so your efforts don't result in a mudslide. Consider not only the depth of the bed but the width as well. Helping to enclose many patios are nice brick planters that are too narrow to grow more than a couple of petunias. Give yourself several feet of width in your planters to create a truly spectacular planting.

A raised bed creates a unique microclimate. The soil in it heats up faster in

From my vantage point inside the summer room, I can spy on Rose, apparently searching for mice.

spring, and thus can be worked sooner. Bulbs planted in raised beds usually bloom before their counterparts in the garden. A bed filled with fresh topsoil makes an ideal growing medium for a vast array of plants. Roses, lilies, and delphiniums—not always happy campers in thick clay—perform like true stars in these custom beds. If you choose to build a series of beds, such as for vegetables or cutting flowers, consider the distance between each bed to provide an adequate path, especially if wheelchairs will need to traverse it. You may decide to

My truck didn't fit inside, so two pairs of French doors and more old porch columns
turned my garage from junk room to summer room.

create a center bed, perhaps highlighted by an arch for roses or morning glories, or a birdbath, with beds radiating away from it.

Before you build, plan your irrigation system for your raised bed. Drip systems and soaker hoses are good options to help you grow healthy plants and conserve water. Because the soil in raised beds heats up, especially if they're constructed of stone or concrete, monitor your beds to make sure they receive adequate moisture.

Penny-Wise and Pond Foolish

Aside from roses, which every novice wants to grow in the worst way (and usually does), ponds are at the top of the wish list for new gardeners. Especially in the heat of summer, a water feature provides a cooling, soothing respite. It opens a whole other dimension in gardening—that of aquatic plants and animals. My animals have always liked my ponds, whether for drinking or an occasional swim for the dogs or as MTV for cats, where swimming goldfish mesmerize them for hours on end. Water lilies and lotus bewitch us completely, and visions of a placid pond surface covered with their flowers may blind us to the actual forethought and expense a pond might entail.

As the veteran of several pond projects, I can warn you that the road from dream to execution can be tricky. And it's difficult to pull off a nice pond or pool with the obligatory waterfalls or fountains without the whole thing looking cheesy. Indeed, some of the most elaborate, most expensive ponds end up being the cheesiest.

The problem starts with the concept. Unless you actually live in the woods or on a mountainside, it's extremely difficult to create a naturalistic water feature. There's no way that any passersby to my garden would believe that I have an outcrop of lichen-covered rocks and a natural spring here on a very flat city block. So if you buy one of the preformed, kidney-shaped pond kits, don't expect you or anyone else will believe it either. If, on the other hand, the land where you garden actually has natural contours and features, make the most of them. Making ponds is for people who actually like and understand plumbing and electricity. You can do it inexpensively, digging the pond yourself and lining it with pliable, durable, heavy-gauge plastic and running cords and outlets to operate the pumps and fountains. It's all very exciting as well as potentially frustrating as you search for a tiny leak where you accidentally punctured the liner.

Many people hire pond specialists. They create and install ponds complete with fish and plants. This costs lots of money and you're suddenly in charge of an ecosystem of which you know little. At once you're faced with algae bloom, dead fish, and mosquito outbreaks. I once dug, lined, and landscaped a pond on live TV during the morning news. People had written in why they wanted and deserved a pond. As I worked, the station checked in with me periodically to watch my progress. It was a horrible two hours, but I got it done and it looked lovely at our 8:45 finale. Water trickled softly down a stone ledge into the clean water where fish swam lazily among the water plants. (It cost about $500, by the way, excluding my labor.) Later that summer I was in the neighborhood and decided to check on my pretty little pond. If the creature from the black lagoon had risen from the muck I wouldn't have been surprised. Needless to say, wanting and deserving a pond didn't necessarily translate into actually caring for one.

I'm telling you this because for every successful pond, there are a dozen others that have been filled in and sodded over. But don't let me dissuade you. Just be prepared to go through an extensive learning process.

One type of water feature that I highly recommend is a self-contained recirculating fountain. All you do is fill it and plug it in. I paid about $200 for mine, a simple little fountain with a verdigris finish. Water trickles into a small bowl just the right size for sparrows and finches that frequent it. If you want birds to use your "drinking fountain," don't add bleach to keep the water clean as is frequently recommended. Just drain and clean it once in a while. In winter, I haul my little fountain inside to my sunroom, where it makes a nice sound and perhaps adds a bit of humidity to the air.

There are so many beautiful fountains available, from classic to contemporary, that you'll find one perfectly suited to your architecture. There are even small, "table top" models for small-space or balcony gardeners. Prices vary, of course, but it's worth searching until you find one that you know is right. If you buy one from a nursery that offers dozens of kinds (all splashing away at the same time), ask them if they can turn off the power so you can hear each one individually. Sound is one of the most important functions of a water feature. Make sure you don't take home a noisy one that forces you to holler as if you're eating dinner at Niagara Falls. My best words of advice on the issue, however, are to select a well-proportioned, nicely designed piece that you'll find just as pleasing next year and the next. That's the trick with artistic pieces.

Garden Art

Over the years, friends have presented me with a variety of garden "art." An assortment of squirrels, bunnies, dragons, plaques, and giant snails has been bestowed upon me. I accept them with as much grace as I can muster, mentally trying to come up with an inconspicuous spot to display them. A fast-growing rampant vine is the best companion.

Visitors have sometimes made the mistake of admiring one of these objets d'art and craft. When they say something like "What a cute ceramic toadstool," I immediately thrust it into their hands with, "Then I insist you take it." I don't take no for an answer, even following them down the street in case they chuck it out their car window.

Americans have had an odd obsession with garden art for many years. Pink flamingos, petunia-planted toilets, and lawn jockeys are our legacy. Even the British, whom we admire for their tasteful pastel perennial borders, litter their gardens with gnomes. I don't get it.

Ponds can be expensive but it's possible to get the soothing sound of splashing water with a relatively inexpensive fountain. Sparrows perch on the rim.

Opening up the summer room with French doors inspired me to build a new patio glowing with mums, hibiscus, and Cape fuchsia.

Garden art doesn't have to be kitschy. It can truly enhance the ambience of a garden. I'm all in favor of a functional ornament such as a well-designed bird-bath. It's worth investing in one good piece rather than a lot of cheap junk. My simple, cobalt blue ceramic version is positioned under an iron trellis on which I grow blue morning glories. It's a destination for the well-groomed robins and jays of the neighborhood. This birdbath has become a focal point rather than an eyesore.

I especially like the sort of granite or marble statues that I can't afford. Posi-tioning them—or any ornament—is key. Ideally, an ornament should complement your plants, not dominate them or substitute for them. Sculpture or fountains can serve as focal points, perhaps drawing the eye down a path or drawing attention to an architectural feature such as a trellis, arbor, or alcove. Conversely, these objects can be placed in such a way that they are to be discovered, nestled with groups of potted plants or amongst woodland plants in a shady setting.

Natural materials in neutral colors, such as wood and stone, belong with plants and flowers. Iron and copper ornaments also age to a pleasing weathered patina. Even well designed concrete objects may become charming garden additions. You can age them prematurely by sponging them with paint in grimy colors as I did with my plastic pots. Many of us find interesting weathered objects in antique stores and architectural salvage yards. These pieces have character and unique qualities that mass-produced objects lack.

Many artists create lovely and often useful objects for your garden. You'll find tiles, hummingbird feeders, obelisks, lanterns, and sculptures at galleries and garden centers. I've even seen interesting wind chimes that make pleasant sounds, even though I have a long-standing aversion to them. I used to live in a little Victorian house next to a ten-story apartment building. Nearly every balcony that faced my backyard had its own wind chime and, on breezy days, the tinkling drove me mad. I was in wind chime hell.

Resources

- Garage sales
- Friends, neighbors, and families
- Alleys
- Attics
- Thrift stores
- Garden clubs and societies
- Seed and nursery catalogs
- Your local garden centers

When a garden object catches your eye and you're tempted to buy it, ask yourself if you'll still like it in three months, let alone three years. If this object is brighter than the flowers you grow, pass on it: plastic and flowers are a poor fit. By all means avoid plaques with quaint sayings; they're as tacky as a "bless this mess" sign over the kitchen sink. And if an object makes a noise—especially a tinkling one—think twice, especially if you live in my neighborhood.

Final Thoughts

Gardening on a shoestring is about more than saving money. It's about the creative use of resources. We've all become accustomed to relying on the old axiom, "You get what you pay for." It's not always true, and that dangling preposition has always annoyed me. In gardening, you get much more than what you paid. Seeds and plants respond to light, warmth, and water, not dollar bills.

I once toured a garden on which the owners had spent an astounding amount of money (in excess of a million dollars, so we were told). It was astoundingly dull. A fellow designer strolling with me summed it up by saying, "All that cash—for so little effect." Apparently money not only can't buy happiness, it can't even get you a pretty garden in which to be miserable. I can only speculate that had the owners taken a small plot on their estate and dug soil, sown seeds, planted, hoed, weeded, and watered, they may have created something about which they could be truly happy. That's just my judgment, of course. To be fair, I don't enjoy my sofa any less because I didn't construct it or the carpet beneath it because I didn't weave it.

For the right person, the process of gardening is what brings satisfaction. Like any pursuit, learning the hows and whys is part of the pleasure. My garden continuously teaches me something new. I'm thrilled (and relieved) when things go according to plan. If things don't work out as I'd envisioned, I want to know why. I loathe killing plants. Ninety-nine out of a hundred times something I did or didn't do causes the loss. Wrong spot. Too much water. Not enough. Mealybug infestation I didn't catch in time. But the more I garden and observe the results, the better those results become.

In just the past year, I've learned some new things about my plants and garden. Potted cyclamens, it seems, don't necessarily need a dormant period as I'd always been told. On a bright windowsill, they will continue to grow and flower if not watered to death. Coral bells don't need as much water as I was giving them since several rotted off at the base. An anti-dessicant spray does wonders to get dwarf

'Black Magic' elephant's ears pair with brilliant 'Sedona' coleus.
Pretty gardens are the product of creativity and sweat.

Late bloomers such as Colchicum autumnale
mark the season finale in my garden in grand style.

Alberta spruces and other evergreens through the winter without sunburning. Baking soda mixed with aloe vera sap really takes away the pain after picking up a hot pan. Non-hardy succulents (that I mistakenly left outside long after everything else had been brought indoors for the winter) can survive many more degrees of frost—ten, actually—than I'd thought possible. Cheap discount store sheets are just as effective for covering plants during the first frost as Ralph Lauren sheets. I could go on, but my editor has enough trouble suppressing my ramblings.

Gardening is a never-ending adventure. As your skills and knowledge expand, you'll surely discover any number of ways to make more beauty on a budget. Good plantsmanship (or plantswomanship) trumps a bankroll every time. Would we all like a million-dollar garden? Absolutely. We'll get there—on a shoestring.

Glossary

amendment—an addition to soil such as manure or compost to enhance its capability to grow certain types of plants.

annual—a plant that completes its life cycle in one growing season; the plants that fit this classification vary by region, such as a geranium that may perform as an annual in cold-winter regions, but lives many years in a warm-winter region.

anther—the pollen-bearing part of the flower.

bare-root—a plant around whose roots the soil has been removed, usually for transplanting or shipping

basal leaves—the foliage at the base of the plant at soil level.

biennial—plants that complete their life cycle in two growing seasons, generally germinating and producing leaves in the first year and flowers and seeds in the second.

border—an area, usually long and straight, that displays a collection of garden plants, as in a perennial border or mixed border.

bulb—the underground storage unit of a plant that contains an embryonic plant inside, such as tulip or lily.

cold-tolerance—the ability of a plant to withstand cool growing conditions, such as spinach and other early-season vegetables.

compost—organic matter, usually garden debris, that has partially decomposed and is used as a soil amendment.

corm—a bulbous underground storage unit without an embryonic plant typified by gladiolus.

cutting—a piece of plant stem rooted in soil or water to produce a new plant.

deadhead—to remove faded flowers on a plant before they form seeds.

direct sowing—planting seeds in the ground rather than in containers to transplant into the ground later.

division—propagating a plant by cutting or pulling its root-ball into two or more sections.

eye—the point on a plant, such as on a potato, from which new growth emerges.

forcing—potting and chilling spring-flowering bulbs to bloom ahead of their counterparts in the ground.

friability; friable—the characteristic of soil that is composed of large organic particles that make it loose and easy to dig.

ground cover—relatively short, spreading perennial plants, often used to advantage in large areas to suppress weeds.

growing zones—designations by the USDA based on climate—especially winter cold—that help gardeners decide which plants will survive and thrive in their gardens.

harden off—gradually exposing greenhouse-grown plants to outdoor conditions.

hardiness—the ability of a plant to withstand extremes, usually in terms of winter cold.

heirloom—a species or variety of plant popular in the past but still grown today; this generally signifies plants cultivated fifty or more years ago.

hybrid—a plant created by crossing two or more species that incorporates the distinct characteristics of each.

leaf axil—the point of a stem or branch from which the leaf emerges.

leaf scald—the browning or burning of foliage by direct sunlight, usually caused by exposing greenhouse-grown plants to sun without a gradual process.

naturalistic garden—a planting scheme that strives to emulate nature, usually with native plants of a region.

offset—a method of propagation by some plants that creates small, identical plants that can be removed and grown; spider plants and aloes form easy-to-spot offsets.

perennial—a plant that survives for three or more years by means of roots that produce new growth each spring, generally after a winter dormancy; perennials do not have the woody structure that shrubs and trees do.

propagate—to grow new plants by such methods as seeding, cuttings, or division.

rhizome—a modified bulbous underground storage system of essentially swollen roots, typified by bearded iris.

root-ball—the root system of a plant.

rooting hormone—a powdered supplement brushed on stem cuttings before inserting them in soil that aids in the formation of new roots.

root rot—usually fatal disease of plant roots caused by wet soil and the resultant lack of oxygen.

rose hip—swollen, attractive, usually red seedpod produced by many roses.

seedpod—protective case containing one or more seeds.

self-sow—unaided propagation by plants themselves.

setting bud—reaching a state of growth at which a plant begins to flower.

soil amendments—See "amendment."

species—distinct, unique life forms; in gardening, species often refer to plants identical to those found in the wild, unaltered by hybridization or selection.

sport—a cultivated plant that differs from the norm, exhibiting a change such as variegated leaves or atypical flower color.

striking a cutting—the process of producing new plants from cuttings; a cutting has struck at the point where new roots form.

subspecies—variant from a recognized species that may display a difference in size or color; generally caused by geographic separation from the original population of plants.

taprooted—characteristic of a plant that is noted for a strong, single root

topdressing—the practice of applying a soil amendment, usually compost, to the top of the soil around the base of plants.

tuber—modified root that stores nutrients underground; dahlias and potatoes grow from tubers.

tuna quarters—nursery slang for small pots containing young plants and measuring 2¼ inches across.

variegation—contrasting patterns on leaves, usually streaks or flecks.

variety—a plant that is grown for its unique characteristics that differ from the species, often the result of "sports."

xeric—a type of plant able to withstand low water intake.

xeriscape—planting featuring plants with low water requirements, capable of growing with little or no supplemental moisture.

Index

Note: page numbers in *italics* indicate illustrations.